TALENT IS NOT ENOUGH

Books for Young People by Mollie Hunter

TALENT IS NOT ENOUGH

MOLLIE HUNTER
on Writing for Children

A Harper Trophy Book
Harper & Row, Publishers

ACKNOWLEDGMENTS

"Talent Is Not Enough," the *May Hill Arbuthnot Honor Lecture*, is reprinted by permission of the American Library Association from the June 1975 issue of *Top of the News*, pages 391–406. Copyright © American Library Association 1975. "Shoulder the Sky" was delivered on May 1, 1975, as The New York Public Library's annual Anne Carroll Moore Lecture. It was originally published as "Shoulder the Sky: On the Writing of Historical Fiction for Children" in the *Bulletin of The New York Public Library* (volume 79, number 2 [Winter 1976] 124–138) and is reprinted with permission. "One World" was delivered on April 29, 1975, at the Enoch Pratt Free Library, Baltimore, Maryland. It was originally published in *The Horn Book* (December 1975 and February 1976 issues). © 1975 by Mollie Hunter. The remaining two sections were also originally lectures given in various American and British universities, libraries, and colleges of education.

Library of Congress Cataloging in Publication Data
McIlwraith, Maureen Mollie Hunter McVeigh, 1922–
   Talent is not enough.

   Bibliography: p.
   Contents: Heins, P. Introduction.—Talent is not enough.—Shoulder the sky. [etc.]
   1. Children's literature—History and criticism—Addresses, essays, lectures.   I. Title.
PN1009.A1M235 1976   808'.068   76-3841
ISBN 0-06-022649-8
ISBN 0-06-446105-X (pbk.)

First Harper Trophy edition, 1990.

*This book is dedicated
affectionately to my teacher
and friend, George M. Mackenzie.*

Contents

Introduction

Mollie Hunter is best known for her historical narratives and fantasies for young people, but her present essays, originally delivered as lectures, pertain to the writing of any work of fiction, juvenile or adult. This gifted practitioner of the art of writing children's books assumes that there are natural and necessary connections linking the various areas of all good writing. She traces the filaments binding folklore to storytelling, storytelling to the experiences of an author, and an author's experiences to the sudden apprehensions often kindled by words in both writers and children.

In *A Sound of Chariots*, Mollie Hunter tells how Bridie McShane, overwhelmed by grief at the death of her father, became suddenly, instantly aware of her physical surroundings, "because through all her senses she was filtering into their component parts the whole vast complex of smells and sounds, shapes, colors and textures through which she moved." And she realized that she too must one day die, and her fear of death became intensified "by the fear of the passage of Time along the way."

From the various allusions to Mollie's own childhood experiences in "Talent Is Not Enough," it becomes obvious that *A Sound of Chariots* is autobiographical. But more significant is Mollie Hunter's observation that "the range of a child's emotion has the same extent as that of an adult, and all the child lacks, by comparison, is the vocabulary to match his range." Bridie's emotions and experiences were obviously Mollie's own emotions and experiences, recollected—not necessarily in tranquillity, but certainly with intensity and with a hard-won power to convey that intensity in words.

Americans should feel gratified that Mollie Hunter, an ardent Scot culturally as well as politically, borrowed a concept from Emerson not only for the title of her first essay but for the overall theme of her book: "Talent alone cannot make a writer. There must be a man behind the book." Mollie Hunter makes the point that "only when a gift for children's writing is allied to accomplished technique, to passion, and to insight, will it produce the highest expression of this, as of any other art." In looking for the person behind the book, the reader of *Talent Is Not Enough* will scarcely be surprised to find a wealth of revelation—autobiographical, emotional, scholarly, intuitive—about Mollie Hunter herself.

The variety, richness, and complexity of the topics she deals with are all part of her life, her art, her personality: Reality, history, and fantasy are allowed to impinge on one another, to create the form of an ultimate synthesis. In "One World," Mollie Hunter indicates the historical, anthropological, and linguistic sources of folklore and reminds us that legend is often no more than reality transformed into something singularly rich and strange. But when she wrote *A Stranger Came Ashore*, a story built around the legends of the Selkie Folk, she endowed it with stormy power and uncanny mystery by seeing the events clairvoyantly through the eyes of Robbie Henderson, her young protagonist.

When Mollie Hunter discusses contemporary realistic fiction for children in the title essay, she mentions the necessity for both emotional and intellectual "frame[s] of reference." The same principle of reference, of significant relationship, is seen at work in a story where folklore and fantasy break through the carefully observed and detailed events.

The whole collection of essays is an extraordinary combination of various patterns of thought and expression. Anecdotes and stories are frequently used to introduce or to illustrate a point. The general discussions of realistic and historical fiction, as well as of fantasy, are significant in their own right, but they are further enhanced by the author's feeling of responsibility toward children's literature. And her intuitive and poetic perceptions reveal her love of words and her constant desire to tell a story.

Although Mollie Hunter's stories are rooted in Scottish soil and history, the range of her fiction is wide-reaching in its sweep and universality; and, in a sense, her essays are confident assertions in another medium of what she does so well in storytelling. It is worth recalling what some of these accomplishments are. *The Lothian Run* and *A Pistol in Greenyards* suggest the novels of Sir Walter Scott for the richness of their historical and narrative textures, and in many ways they are more immediate in their present-day appeal than the works of her great predecessor. *The Kelpie's Pearls*, *Thomas and the Warlock*, and *A Stranger Came Ashore* are extended narratives developed from the fantasy often implicit in folklore. *A Sound of Chariots* is realistic, intense, immediate.

The Stronghold, winner of the Carnegie Medal in 1975, is a superb example of how Mollie Hunter's mind works. In her Foreword to that book, she tells of the "brochs," ancient, massive stone structures found in the north of Scotland, and she conjectures how they were used as a defense against the Roman navy raiding for slaves. Speculating that these structures must have been based on "an idea springing from one brilliant mind," she created Coll, the young, crippled genius who designed them, and then she developed a story that not only tells about the building of the fortifications but also evokes the power and the ceremonies of the Druids.

In real life, Mollie Hunter uncannily fulfills the promise of her books. Energetic, keen, observant, intellectually sensitive, she made an ideal companion on a walking tour of Boston in the spring of 1975. Not a single historical allusion, no item of architectural significance, escaped her attention; and I loved her remark when we came to Chestnut Street, one of the finest streets on Beacon Hill. "I have always wanted a house in Edinburgh and one in the south of France; and now, I also want one on Chestnut Street—that one," she said, and pointed to it.

But all is not flourish or—as she likes to call it—panache with Mollie Hunter. She also has moments of sober insight; and although her intuitions may partake of melancholy, they are, at the same time, heroic and eminently reasonable:

> *To say, then, that the writer's lot is a lonely one is not to complain of this, but simply to make the point that to be creative is to be different from those who are not; and so, to that extent also, to be cut off from those others. Yet, ironically, it is out of this even deeper loneliness that the writer hopes to be able to communicate to an extent denied the non-creative ones; and the irony is accentuated by his awareness that he will never really be able to tell how far he has succeeded in this.*

PAUL HEINS

TALENT
IS NOT
ENOUGH

Foreword

I have the sort of tidy mind that likes to sense a completed pattern of thought; and in the course of delivering the lectures now here published, I was involved in numerous discussions on a main theme currently occupying the minds of many in the children's book world. For the other participants in those discussions, therefore, as well as for myself, it may complete the present pattern if I refer briefly now to that same theme—i.e. what may or should form the content of children's books.

There are certain enduring factors in writing for children. That, at least, is indisputably so; and much of what has been said in the following pages is an attempt to delineate these factors. Their nature is enduring because it answers to requirements which are complementary to one another—namely, the specifications needed to create literature, and an awareness of what will best feed the imagination of growing minds.

In the first of these requirements is implicit that a good book for children is simply one which is a good book in its own right, and which should thus also be a source of pleasure, profit, or interest to any adult reader. The converse of this—that any child may derive equal benefit from a book answering to the same definition—is demonstrated untrue by the fact that the second requirement implicitly recognises the limited experience of childhood.

This may seem like stating the obvious; yet it has still to be proved so in the argument between the conservative school of thought which sees itself as protecting the innocence of the young reader, and the avant-garde firmly aligned on the fact that children are inescapably involved in all the brutal realities of adult life. And so, how *are* we finally to assess what is a good book for children? The answer to this may seem to need redefinition with each new generation; yet to my mind, it exists complete and changeless in a phrase coined by that eminent personality of the children's book world, Edward Blishen. A good book which is also truly for children's reading, has *"the child's eye at the centre."*

A marvellous phrase, this! In the idea behind it the experience of the children's writer melds harmoniously with the perception of the child-reader. To encounter that idea is like coming unexpectedly on a photograph of oneself taken in childhood; and looking into those eyes staring big and wondering out of the past, suddenly to know again *exactly* how it felt to be that age. Yet still, with the knowing, comes a rush of pity—as happened once with me, seeing an old group-photograph of schoolchildren.

My own face stared out of the group, earnest, its whole soul in its eyes. I stared back at those eyes, knowing what lay ahead for their unguarded look and thinking desperately, *Warn her! Oh, for God's sake, why did nobody warn her!*

But of course, nobody could have; and for the children to come, nobody ever can—the very inexperience of childhood making it that time of discovery which cannot be lived otherwise than day by day.

I have spoken elsewhere in this book of the technique, the passion, and the insight which must all be allied to the talent of the writer; but there are other needs. There is the honesty to apply that technique solely in terms of that same childhood inexperience; the courage to look out from the story with that same unguarded look. It is only when all these needs are satisfied that the writer will be able genuinely to convey the feelings recalled by that old photograph. And then also, whatever may be the prevailing critical standards for children's books, whatever fashion or prejudice may say of the finished effort, this writer will have created something which can truly be called a children's book—a good one!

Talent
Is Not
Enough

May Hill Arbuthnot
Honor Lecture 1975

Long ago, when I had to endure the kindly, adult condescension that asks, "And what will you be when you grow up?" I used to answer,
"A kennel maid."

They smiled, reading into this only a childish desire to achieve a life-long romp with the more playful versions of man's faithful friend. *I* smiled, letting them have their delusion, the while I gritted my milk-teeth on a private vision of myself as a commanding figure with wrists of steel tautly controlling a pack of huge and baying hounds, a fearless trainer, an expert tracker, a—

"Nonsense!" said a teacher who asked me this same question one day and was given my usual answer. "You'll be a writer." And passed so firmly on to the child next in line of question that there was no arguing with her decision. The idea that I could be a

4

writer was planted in my head; and for this, at least, I must thank that strong-minded lady—although how she had reached so positive a conclusion can only be a guess with me now. I was talkative, of course—I have to admit that; and even at that tender age I was what I have always continued to be—a storyteller with a great love for words of sweet sound and rich colouring. Yet what neither she nor anyone else could have forecast at that time was that these drives would eventually find their true scope in writing for children; and for this, as for every other form of the art, there is a statement by Ralph Waldo Emerson which makes a shot in the dark out of any prediction for a future in writing.

"Talent alone cannot make a writer. There must be a man behind the book."

"A *person* behind the book" would be the more acceptable phrasing nowadays, and—although I have no wish to try to improve on Emerson—it points the reference to say simply that "talent is not enough." This much one learns in writing for children—to be terse without losing the totality of a meaning; and it is in writing for children that I see the deepest implications of the whole statement. I call a ghost to witness the initial proof of this—the fearsome, rheumaticky ghost of the man who was Granpa Cormack.

He was an acquaintance of my village childhood in the Lowlands of Scotland, this old man, and the sphere of his power was the local market garden. He was very tall and thin, with a hobbling walk aided by a long, heavy stick. His face was small and russet-coloured, heavily wrinkled by age, bad temper, and the pain of his rheumatics. Like ourselves, he used the broad Doric, which was the everyday speech of the Lowlands then; and to him, we village children were always "they blawstit bairns"—those damn kids.

Granpa Cormack purely hated children; yet it was to this old curmudgeon we had to apply in the summer holidays for a chance to earn much-needed cash from what we called "a job at the berries," and so Granpa was both our terror and our joy. Terror struck when he came hobbling down the rows of raspberry bushes, roaring, and laying about him with that heavy stick. Joy came in the weighing-house when our berry-picking for the day was checked, wages were paid, and we all scuffled about gleefully trying to confuse Granpa's calculations with practical jokes—such as hiding stones in the baskets to increase their weight, and then stealthily abstracting the same.

It was still from Granpa Cormack, all the same, that I learned to recognise at least one aspect of the truth implicit in my theme, for berry-pickers under his rule were never allowed to do anything in half-hearted fashion. The basket for holding the fruit had to be slung around the neck so that both hands were free to work. Otherwise, like some ancient Demon King shooting through a stage trapdoor, Granpa would burst from the bushes roaring,

"Yase baith eer haunds!"

The English of this is "use both your hands," and

it indicates the basic and very obvious sense in which talent is not enough. Even the greatest talent, lacking the craft to develop it, is no more than an itch in the mind; and the higher the potential, of course, the greater the effort needed to bring it to peak achievement.

To sustain the effort, however, means cultivating the capacity to endure loneliness—not that loneliness itself is peculiar to the creative mind. Far from that, the mere fact of being human implies an essential loneliness in each of us—microcosmic as we all are; for universe may communicate with universe, but by their very nature they cannot mingle.

To say, then, that the writer's lot is a lonely one is not to complain of this, but simply to make the point that to be creative is to be different from those who are not; and so, to that extent also, to be cut off from those others. Yet, ironically, it is out of this even deeper loneliness that the writer hopes to be able to communicate to an extent denied the non-creative ones; and the irony is accentuated by his awareness that he will never really be able to tell how far he has succeeded in this.

A writer, indeed, could be likened to a person locked for life in a cell—someone to whom the mere fact of imprisonment has taught things he wants desperately to convey. He compiles a code, spends the rest of his life using this to tap out messages on the wall of his cell, and all the time he taps he is asking himself,

"Is there anyone out there listening? Can they hear me? Do they understand?"

It may take years of experiment, too, before a writer can even be sure he is using the code which is best for him—before he settles down, in fact, to the form of writing that best deploys his particular talent; and with hindsight on my own experience, I can see nothing to choose between myself and an old shepherd to whom I gave a lift in my car, late one winter's night. He sat watching the road ahead, this old fellow, his gaze fixed on the centre-line of glass studs endlessly reflecting light from the car's headlamps. But seemingly he had not grasped that this *was* simply a repeated reflection, for at last he said in a puzzled voice,

"Wha lichts they?" (Who lights these?)

I explained that the lights were only reflectors set into the road, but he was not convinced by this. Some person or other must have lit the road ahead—he was sure of that; and so it was with me at the start of my career as a children's writer. In spite of the years I had spent learning and attempting to practise the writer's art, I came late to this aspect of it, and only then because of the persuasions of my own two young children. The book they coaxed from me was expanded from stories I had previously made up for them; but for me it was also a sustained attempt at a form of language that could ring true only if it hit a particular note—a traditional note, evolved from many, many past centuries of the music in the story-teller's voice.

I took the children with me on the way to rediscovery of that music, reading the book to them by installments in the course of its writing. And even although I realised it was only the beam of my own imagination reflecting back at me from their pleasure in this tale, I still had the feeling of being on a road where *someone* had placed lights ahead for me.

There was one other thing happened in the course of all this to convince me that this lit road was the one I would travel thenceforth, and always. At a certain point in the story, my eight-year-old son wept—more than that, he wept in a way I had never seen happen before with him, or with any other child. He sat bolt upright, never ceasing to listen to my reading, his gaze never shifting from me. There was no blinking, no sniffling, not a tremor of his features. The tears simply rose up, filled his eyes, then spilled over, and bounced like drops of broken crystal down his cheeks. The child seemed unaware he *was* weeping, in fact; and to me, it was a very moving thing, for spontaneous tears like this come from some suddenly-touched and very deep level of emotion.

I read further on, and the tears no longer came. But duration of an emotion is no gauge of its intensity. Moreover, the range of a child's emotion has the same extent as that of an adult, and all the child lacks, by comparison, is the vocabulary to match his range —yet still there are ways of supplying this defect. So variable are the uses of language, so infinitely flexible their application, that the storyteller may turn the simplest of words into poetry powerful enough to express the deepest, most complex of emotions; and this note of strong and simple poetry was the very one I had been attempting to strike in my choice of language for that particular book.

Those soundless tears, then, did more than move me. I felt them as an honour, for the story situation that drew them was poignant beyond the child's own power to express; but he had understood my form of words for it, and they had spoken for him. And so at last, it seemed to me then, I had discovered my particular code—one that would indulge my keen delight in all the effects of sound and rhythm and meaning in language, as much as it satisfied my instinctive urge to turn everything, everything, *everything*, into a story!

A synthesis of two loves had brought me to this point—my writing and my children. Yet it does not follow that the writer who loves children can or should be a children's writer, any more than that a person who loves animals can or should be a liontamer. Love can be blind, inept, a bore. Understanding is Argus-eyed, and shrewd in realising the child's need for story-characters through whom he can identify with the rest of humankind, and so discover who *he* is, how he "belongs."

Talking of this to my husband one day, he quoted something from his own childhood in the village neighbouring mine—Prestonpans, locally known simply as "the Pans."

When I was a wee lad we used to play at "War"—the First World War, with Germans on one side, British on the other; and the men of the Pans were there in the thick of it, and fighting with the best of them. Then after I went to school and had a history lesson or two, we played at "War" again—Robert the Bruce at Bannockburn, with Scots on one side and the English on the other; and the men of the Pans were in that fight too, and still among the best of them. I never had any trouble in identifying!

And neither he had. A childhood where story was king had seen to that; and in the talent of the children's writer, the lively imagination of the storyteller is the basic and chief ingredient.

A powerful grip on the possibilities of language is also essential in writing for children. This, because selectivity must be practised in relation to the reader's age—which is not to say, of course, that a child should not be sent scurrying to the dictionary for help. Rather, it indicates that, out of all the choices available in a given syntax, the children's writer is constantly being forced to find the simple one which will enhance rather than diminish his text, by being at the same time the strongest, or the most vividly descriptive. The bones of language are what he seeks —spare, smooth, strong, needing no fleshy padding to elaborate a structure already inherently beautiful.

The capacity to recall the sensory impacts and perceptions of one's early years is obviously also a vital part of the talent in question; but a further dimension of recall is needed for the physical world of childhood, which, we tend to forget, is out of scale in surroundings proportioned to adults. Terror, adventure, or interest exist here in direct proportion to this distortion of scale—especially for the very young child, to whom the underside of a table may be a dark cave; a walk of a few yards along a gloomy path a journey of heroic proportions; a scuffle of dust a relief-map, fascinating in its contours, offering godlike opportunities for rearrangement of hills and valleys.

Finally, to come full circle on the question of emotion, adult life conforms to a code that debars spontaneity, and is embarrassed by naked idealism. To scream, shout, or howl to release a feeling is considered uncivilized; to be a committed idealist is thought naive. So adults learn to protect themselves from over-painful realisations, and to blunt the first sharp edge of any emotion; with the result that uninhibited displays of childhood emotion become gradually incomprehensible to them. And so they tend to move through the causes of these with all the expertise of elephants trying to balance on the tips of asparagus fern.

The person whose nature has intended him to be a children's writer can find a way through this delicate jungle, for there is something in that nature which has preserved the child's sense of wonder, and kept alight the enthusiasms of youth. The other side of this coin is that some, at least, of his emotions remain as raw and vulnerable as in those early years; and thus he may feel again the first sharpness of their impact, as much as he is able to re-experience the terror of the dark cave, the gloomy path, to taste and sense again with the novel faculties of youth, and to visualise once more in a careless scuffle of dust the marvellous contours of a small, strange world.

All this may not answer to what children's writers, in fact, are; but that does not invalidate any theory of what their talent should be. The touchstone of truth is in the children themselves; and I look back with gratitude to having my own two children to inform me so. I had another good fortune at that time, however, and that was in having reached a point in my life where I was ready to rebel sharply against all the conventions which then ruled the world of children's writing.

It was wrong and stupid, in my opinion, that this should be dominated by a middle-class syndrome which was no more than a hangover from the days of Victorian nurseries; downright ridiculous that juvenile hero-characters should always be children of this class engineered into excitement through such highly-coincidental unlikelihoods as parents called suddenly to visit sick Aunt Jessie, jewel thieves in the neighbourhood, and the only policeman available being either stupid, deaf, or venal. This was pre-masticated pap, regurgitated for a mythical "child-reader" by adults who were themselves examples of retarded mental development.

In my view also, all those publishers with fixations on stories of English boarding-school life came into this same retarded category. Such stories, I guessed, were more than just alien to my native Scots tradition. They must certainly also be incomprehensible to all children not of the élite minority processed through such unnatural institutions. As a parent, I was angered by the humiliations of poor children perpetually confronted in their reading by the cruel implication that they were the exceptions to the rule of people never having to worry about the rent, or getting enough to eat, or being cold and ragged. As for the historical novels written for children, I considered it was high time someone put paid to all those cardboard figures flouncing about in period dress, and delicately flourishing anachronistic handkerchiefs.

If a seventeenth-century commoner blew his nose with his fingers, let him do that! And why not write about commoners anyway, instead of allowing an endless parade of aristocrats to dominate the scene? Commoners are the very stuff of history. The feel, the taste, the smell of history is what comes through their lives—"the rascal multitude," the canaille—those who beg and starve and steal, or labour skilfully if they have been lucky enough to have the chance of learning a trade; and through the centuries, die in the cannon's mouth. Let them speak, for a change!

So I argued—hotly. But of course, I was only one of a considerable number of authors who were then briskly engaged in freeing the whole scene of children's writing from its artificial conventions; and now this freedom has been so well accomplished that one finds it hard to believe these conventions ever existed. And yet, and yet . . . It cannot be too strongly insisted that freedom is not only a state of being. It is also an attitude of mind. Lacking this, freedom fragments into anarchy—a sequence that impels us from the examination of talent to its place in context of the statement that "talent is not enough."

"There must be a person behind the book" is the corollary to this statement; and sooner or later in a writer's life comes the situation where—like every other individual—he or she is faced with all the implications of his own personality in relation to past events and future possibilities. The confrontation is a painful one, yet without the self-knowledge it brings, there can be no true understanding of other people, no real compassion for them. And to experience these feelings for others is also to experience the sole possible victory over the essential loneliness of the human condition. The victory, however, comes only very gradually, for it relates directly to the slow and difficult process of accepting one's self-knowledge and coming to peaceful terms with it. Sometimes, indeed, the process is lost sight of altogether. Yet still the trigger-point can remain clear in the mind; and I can place exactly when this happened in my own life.

October 1956. The rising of the Hungarian people against Soviet Communist rule. The last, pathetic broadcast to the rest of Europe, asking for the help that never came. The pictured glimpse of a young girl's face—round, serious, innocent, as she marched along under a banner that asked for nothing more than peace and freedom. Another glimpse of the same child—she could not have been more than fifteen—lying dead from machine-gun fire. The heart-breaking message sent with the children rushed out of Budapest and over the Austrian border—*We are staying to fight. Please look after our children.*

We never missed a news broadcast at that time, my husband and I. The tension in our household took on an unbearable edge. Then, at the end of a bulletin one day, the Red Cross made an appeal for people to help in the dangerous work of getting those children over the Austro-Hungarian border, and suddenly I felt a great, cracking release at the very deepest level of my emotions.

Children are important to me. I look at the eyes of an eight-year-old and see a wonder shining there which, in every generation, is innocence renewed; and I am moved to tenderness. I look at the eyes of an adolescent and see there the conflicting eagerness and uncertainty of the between years; and I find myself touched by a strong compassion.

My own two children were the most important things in the world to me at that time. My love for my husband was deep. My fear of death for myself was an obsession which had haunted me every day from the moment when the death of my father—loved to the point of idolatry—had shattered my nine-year-old life. Yet in that sudden moment of emotional release, nothing of all this mattered any more. My loves were unaltered, I was still desperately afraid of dying, but I knew I had to do *something* to save even one at least of those child victims—anything at all, supposing it was only protecting the child from death with my own body. Otherwise, I realised, I would either have to live with the memory of a betrayal; or, like Judas, go hang myself, for I could never bear to look myself in the face again.

I told my husband I was going straight out to answer the Red Cross appeal. I can see yet his look of sadness; but he was—and is—a man of conscience, and he made no attempt to stop me. And so off I went to volunteer—and found my noble gesture ending in bathos, for I had none of the special skills the Red Cross work needed, and another dead body would have been only an embarrassment to them.

My offer of help was not accepted; yet still my moment of self-confrontation retained its value, for out of it I had learned that there are worse things in life than dying, and that some things are worth dying for.

I found myself looking at my life with new eyes, the eyes of self-knowledge. I began the painful process of coming to terms with what I saw, of developing some philosophy out of it; and because I am a writer, the maturing of such talent as I had ran parallel to this process. In time, some aspect or other of this slowly-forming philosophy became integral to everything I wrote; and so in time also, I arrived at my final clear criteria for deciding what place to assign the terms "suitable" and "unsuitable" in children's reading.

I recall an old Scots lady who told me scathingly, "Ach books! If ye've read yin, ye've read the lot!"

I challenge anyone to produce a comment more shattering to a writer, or more ignorant of the true and ultimate function of books—which is to preserve aspects of life conveyed in terms of enduring importance, creative imagination, and artistic skill. This is the dictionary definition of literature, but it should be remembered that these same aspects include high adventure, humour, and fantasy—as instanced, say, in R.L. Stevenson's *Treasure Island*, Mark Twain's *Tom Sawyer*, and James Stephens' *The Crock of Gold*. All of these were beloved books of my own childhood. All answer truly to the definition of literature. With them, for example, it could reasonably be argued that children are as entitled as adults to the benefits of so valuable a human endeavour—more so, indeed, for the first light of literature on a young mind does more than illumine. A touch of glory descends, and that mind can never be truly dark again.

No such argument is needed, of course, for the child whose reading ability has outstripped his physical age. For this reader, at least, any book which yields something of literary value is a suitable one; but by far the greater number of children will find their reading pleasure in books which take account of the general limitations of childhood's intellectual experience, and which are therefore categorised as being specifically for certain age groups.

A dual onus thus falls on those who provide the normal reading experience of children. They must ensure that this offers literature in the fullest meaning of that word, and they must bear in mind that children are—or should be—a special care; in the sense that literature is one of the mediums through which young minds eventually reach maturity. Thus also, if old conventions are to be discarded as restrictive to the true function of literature as well as being socially outmoded, they must be replaced by at least this one all-important convention—the convention of care; and the only area of debate left is the extent of this care and the manner in which it should be demonstrated.

At first sight the answer seems obvious and very simple. No single group of people has the right to ignore a consensus of thoughtful opinion on the development of the child mind; particularly where this is concerned with the comparative defencelessness of the pre-pubertal years. Some form of censorship would therefore appear to be a continuing need—a sort of gentle conspiracy, perhaps, of adults who are socially progressive, well-intentioned, and experienced in the world of children's books; but this will not do. It will never do, or we shall be back where we started with the new freedom simply recreating the old prison in modern shape.

On the other hand, there are themes now encountered in children's books which, at first mention, appear totally unsuitable for readers of tender age. To name but a few at random—race prejudice, social deprivation, drug usage and abusage, environmental pollution—all of which are topics of burning relevancy to our society; and all of which, once the shock of first mention is past, can be seen to affect the lives

19

of children as much as they affect the lives of adults. Inevitably, therefore, it must be accepted that children have to learn to relate to the type of situation from which such themes are drawn; but the operative phrase which defines the convention of care in this respect is that they should be enabled to do so *in a manner that raises the level of their understanding.*

Thus, for the children's writer who chooses any such theme, there is only one way of discharging his dual onus. He must create some frame of reference which will enable the reader to relate intellectually to the *significance* of that theme; and the same pattern of argument applies to themes of an emotional significance.

A broken home, the death of a loved person, a divorce between parents—all these are highly-charged emotional situations once considered unsuitable for children's reading, but which are nevertheless still part of some children's experience; and the writer's success in casting them in literary terms rests on the ability to create an emotional frame of reference to which children in general can relate.

The new freedom of the children's writer, in fact, would appear to have no problems that talent and technique combined cannot solve. It gives the impression of youth itself—expansive, strong, vigorous. Yet the impression is mistaken, for this particular freedom is a delicate thing. Like a small, wild bird, its wings are easily broken. It can be killed by capture.

Where is the emotional frame of reference for rape? Or for baby-battering? More often than we care to think, the rapist's victim is a child. The incidence of children maimed or beaten to death by a violent parent has been revealed as wide-spread in western society. Are we to infer here also that we are justified in arguing from the particular to the general—that because some children are victims of such aberrant behaviour, it may be made part of all children's experience? The examples chosen are not extreme, and it would be absurd for the children's writer to beg this question and yet still claim free choice of thematic material.

Similarly, where is the intellectual frame of reference for all the decadent aspects of our society—the hedonism, the perversions of art and nature, the dance on the edge of the grave that flaunts the triumph of sensation over sensitivity? To pretend unawareness of these is in itself a form of decadence. Not to condemn them also as being aberrations from even our wildly imperfect norm is to live without courage—worse, without hope for the future. And children *are* the future. Are we, then, justified in sending them out with minds crippled by our own handicaps?

The distinction between the normal and the aberrant—this, to my mind, is where the dividing line should be drawn in themes for children's writing, with all that lies on the side of the normal classed as suitable, and all on the other side as unsuitable. This, it seems to me, is where the convention of care must operate most strongly—particularly in those tender pre-pubertal years. Otherwise, the law of diminishing returns is immediately activated, and the writer will only succeed in rubbing his young reader's nose in the dirt of the world before the same child has had the chance to realise that the world itself is a shining star.

It could be fairly argued, of course, that there is no need for any such dividing line; the good taste of either writer or publisher, or of both combined, making a sufficient safeguard to the rights and sensibilities of young readers. I would not wish to be Cassandra in this, for it could be just as fairly argued that those of a generation ago made the same assumption on matters they considered unsuitable for children's reading; and their mould was rudely broken.

It would be a very blinkered approach which did not recognise that ours could be broken as rudely—and not least because the new freedom of children's writers has also meant new scope for talented people in every aspect of the children's book world. In effect, children's writing is rapidly rising from its position as the Cinderella of the arts; and it could be salutary to wonder whether some talented newcomers to the ball might be more concerned with dancing in glass slippers than with keeping an ear open for the midnight chime that warns, *Children . . . ! Children . . . !*

The law of diminishing returns will begin to operate with a vengeance then—indeed, the conditions for it seem already to have been set to some extent by the technical device so often now used to define the frame of reference for a realistic story of modern times. This is the first-person narrative, in which the limits of a young narrator's grasp are set as those presumed for the young reader. The result of this device may be a story to which a reader can relate in very direct terms; but simply because of the narrator's limited vocabulary, there is no scope for the adventure in language which allows the reader's mind to soar. And overall, this is a loss.

In terms of an individual book, this net loss may be small. In terms of a vogue, or cult, in children's books, the loss could be significant; and at the present time, it seems to me that the vogue in "realistic" stories for children is indeed beginning to take on the aspect of a cult. This in turn could spell out the danger of even greater loss than an incidental restriction on language—the danger that children over-burdened by serious themes may be made old before their time; or even, simply, that they may be denied the due need of their natural fascination for the fantastic, the hilarious, the exotic, the adventurous, in storytelling.

These are all items that have to be taken into account before the freedom of the children's writer can be assessed for what it truly is—freedom with responsibility. They are only one more aspect of the convention of care; and it is only by respecting that convention that this same freedom can be exercised in a manner which has value to the development of a particular age group, at the same time as it sustains the concept of literature.

One last point must be made. There can never be any question, in all this, of preaching to the young. That would not only be self-defeating, in the sense that it would produce a tract instead of literature. It would also be a useless exercise—as both argument convinces, and vivid recollections of my own childhood remind me.

I had the run of my grandfather's library then—a collection devoted to works of an "improving" nature, but the only improvement this achieved for me was that I learned to read very fast. I had to, in order to be able to pick out the action scenes from the long, moralising passages I thought of as "the dull bits." My Puritan upbringing balanced the account with feelings of guilty unease over deceiving poor grandfather. Yet despite the guilt, I still resented the dull bits as attempts to lecture me about life, when what I wanted to do was to find out about it for myself. And this latter, it seems to me, is the driving urge of the older child whose basic need to identify has to take account of the expanding realisations of his adolescent years.

The world to be faced then, this adolescent becomes vaguely aware, is more complex than he had imagined in the years of early childhood. Right and wrong, good and evil, are no longer absolutes, in the sense that different groups of people have differing interpretations of these terms. Vaguely also, he senses that his very freedom of choice as an individual is forcing him to decide with which group he will stand; and here, it also seems to me, is the important area in which the convention of care must operate for such readers.

To "load" the story in favour of the writer's own standards would be morally wrong and eventually as self-defeating as preaching at the reader—who would very quickly detect any atmosphere of special pleading. And yet the children's writer who aims a story at this particular age group is opting out of his responsibilities as a person unless he acknowledges the type of dilemma which can face its members. And once again, any talent which cannot make this acknowledgment in story terms must yield any claim to create literature.

I recall one book in particular which faced me with problems on all the counts I have mentioned, but specifically on this last one. It concerned certain true incidents of witchcraft in sixteenth-century Scotland, and was published at a time when witchcraft was much in vogue as a subject; but this last, so far as I was concerned, was simply coincidence. My interest was in the personal and historical motivations behind these incidents; yet how could I convey this interest to young readers either through people so depraved as the witches themselves, or as brutal as those who eventually brought them to justice?

I found the key to my problem in two characters. Without loss of historical accuracy, I could picture one of the witches as a young girl drawn unwillingly into conspiracy. Without any distortion of actual events, I could create the fictitious character of a boy through whom her story was told. By using this latter device, moreover, I would be projecting through a character who was only an accidental witness to the activities of the witches; and so, without in any way minimising the degree of their depravity, I could be selective in terms of the incidents witnessed and the nature of such incidents.

Thus far the technical expertise of my craft had carried me; yet still I knew that to write this book in terms of incident only would be a sterile exercise— the very manipulation of acquired skills I so despised. I had to get behind the eyes of my characters, find the little threads of common human feeling that bound them to me, not as a writer, but as a person. I had to discover from this something that was worth writing about, or the book would not be worth writing at all.

What sort of people were my girl, Gilly, and my young fellow, Adam? I had visualised her as a victim, a gentle creature without the courage to fight against her fate. I had made him sullen, aggressive; someone who believed he could survive his own brutal circumstances only by treating pity for others as a sign of weakness in himself. What happens when the lives of two such youngsters become entangled?

Would not Adam then face a choice? Would he not have to show himself more than ever ruthless; or, even if it meant lessening the chances of his own survival, to allow himself to feel compassion for Gilly? As a writer, I knew I could achieve greater depth of characterisation for Adam if I had him choose the latter course; and that this would also create insight on all the other characters involved with him. As a person, I had learned that only in compassion is true strength; and thus Adam's struggle towards the same knowledge became the pivot on which the whole plot turned.

I enjoyed writing that book. There is a particular exhilaration in voicing a belief passionately held; an exquisite pleasure in practising a craft learned only very slowly to the point where the skills are confidently handled. I was confident enough at that time to feel I could give my story the bite and pace it needed, and through the reluctant growth of Adam's compassion for Gilly, I spoke out loud and clear.

But to what purpose? Was there anyone out there listening? Could they hear me? Did they understand?

One looks around in schools and libraries at children in the teen years, and the exaltation of writing is overtaken by forlorn realism. In general, one must acknowledge, the minds of these children are preoccupied with the myriad trivia of their days. In particular, the physical uncertainties of adolescence have brought each one to the peak point of self-obsession normally experienced in an individual life. What time or inclination have they for an appreciation of literature? How capable are they of such an appreciation?

The honest answer to both questions is that the majority of these young people will always read at the superficial level, and it will always be incident which has the predominant impact on their minds.

The characterisation which dictates course and development of incident will always be taken for granted, *but*—and here, ah here, one may soar again! Even the most superficial reader will follow the incident by identifying with the character concerned in it; and so, willy-nilly, there comes a point when reader and character are involved in the same emotions.

The experience does not last, of course—how long does it take to read a book? Yet even so, the reader will at least have glimpsed a reflection of himself in another young person caught in a situation that demands the enunciation of some value, the setting of some standard. Temporarily at least, he will have had a sense of participating in the decision taken, and the process of thought set subconsciously in train may yet surface in his mind. Moreover, if the writer has done his job properly *as* a writer, story will still be king. And so the reader will still be essentially free to formulate his own eventual philosophy; but the convention of care will at least have shown him something of what may be implied by the choices occurring in those adolescent years.

"It all sounds very moral." This was the comment made to me in a rather dismissing manner on another occasion when I put forward these ideas; and yet what is their obvious alternative? The theory that the artist owes allegiance to nothing save his art?

This is no more than a time-worn excuse invented for the credulous by the inadequate, for the essence of creativeness is the ability to produce a work which is more than the sum of its parts. The artist's own life is only one of the many lives which form these parts, and the basis of his achievement is in realising and accepting his involvement with those others. Its significance is in having transmuted this acceptance into a form which has beauty and meaning for them also.

Any other claim for the artist is sheer humbug, for not to accept involvement is to admit to a talent too feeble to direct the true springs of creativity. Where children are concerned, it is pernicious humbug, for children have no experience against which they may assess the artifice of such a claim. They have not yet learned what it is to ask for bread, and be given a stone. And so, perhaps it *is* all very moral; yet not, I think, in the way the commentator implied.

The eye of self-knowledge informs me that such values as I have are not mine by right. Nor have I done anything to earn my basic abilities as a writer. All these are part of something life has given me; therefore something I owe. And what I owe I must give back, along with the natural increase due to experience. This, it seems to me, is merely what honesty demands; and true honesty is itself the only true morality. I find my way of giving through children, because I am a children's writer, and because no comment on childhood has ever moved me so much as these lines from G.K. Chesterton's poem "The Nativity":

> *Have a myriad children been quickened,*
> *Have a myriad children grown cold,*
> *Grown gross, and unloved, and embittered,*

Grown cunning, and savage, and old.
God abides in a terrible patience,
Unangered, and unworn,
And again, for the child that was squandered,
A child is born.

What a catalogue of blame! And what a note of grace at its end.

The child that was myself was born with a little talent, and I have worked hard, hard, hard, to shape it. Yet even this could not have made me a writer, for there is no book can tell anything worth saying unless life itself has first said it to the person who conceived that book. A philosophy *has* to be hammered out, a mind shaped, a spirit tempered. This is true for all of the craft. It is the basic process which must happen before literature can be created. It is also the final situation in which the artist is fully fledged; and because of the responsibilities involved, these truths apply most sharply to the writer who aspires to create literature for children.

Especially for this writer, talent is not enough—no, by God it is not! Hear this, critics, editors, publishers, parents, teachers, librarians—all you who will shortly pick up a children's book to read it, or even glance idly through it. There *must* be a person behind that book.

Shoulder
the Sky

Anne Carroll Moore
Lecture 1975

The troubles of our proud and angry dust,
Are from eternity, and shall not fail.
Bear them we can; and if we can, we must,
Shoulder the sky, my lad, and drink your ale. *

Who are we, this "proud and angry dust"? Whence
are we? How may we relate to one another, young to
old, race to race, nature to nature? And when do we
feel the first glimmer of curiosity that prompts us to
ask such questions?

I was three years old when my great-grandmother
Hunter first talked and sang to me of the lawless
forays carried out by the men that Scotland knew
long ago as "the Border reivers." She was ninety-
three, her voice long since cracked and wasted, but

*A.E. Housman, *Last Poems*

there was still a wild, strange music in the very names I heard from her—Kerr, Elliot, Graham, Hunter, Armstrong. . . .

"And you're an Elliot, as well as a Hunter," she told me. "You have the Elliot nose." Which is perfectly true, if unenviable; this feature being somewhat less than handsome. Yet still I recall the marvellous thrill of discovery it gave, to put my hand up then and there, and for the first time realise my nose as a distinctive promontory that gave some sort of meaning to my face, and so to me as an entity; as a person.

"Tell us about the olden days," my own family begged me constantly when they were children—anything before their own time being "the olden days." And so I told them of my own childhood in a small village of Lowland Scotland—of the smell of hot, fresh bread wafting from the bakery door in the dark of a winter's morning, of watching the blacksmith heat the iron rim of a wheel red-hot in his forge, of ploughmen dancing in hobnailed boots at the "kirn" that celebrated the end of harvest, of games played in the churchyard where once—long ago—witches had also danced, and where the effigies of Crusading knights lay with stone swords clasped in quietly-folded hands of stone.

I recreated history for them, in fact—both the personal and the general note of it—in the same way as my great-grandmother had done for me. And listening to me, these latest motes of "proud and angry dust" took their first step to identifying with their own kind in times past. They found their own place in the generation table, felt the firm ground in which their roots grew; and it was from this firm ground they were able eventually to look about them and ask the sort of question that Housman's lines prompted me to ask.

They needed the knowledge of these roots. All children do, before they can orientate themselves, first to the family group, and then to the wider grouping beyond that. The school history lesson is the widened concept of this idea; but learning and realisation do not always relate in their intended form, and this is why there must sometimes also be the chance to follow a different drum—one that beats with the enticing sound and surge of story weaving through the grey haze of times that otherwise refuse to come alive.

This is where the historical novelist may be acknowledged as coming into his or her own—always provided he or she is not of the pseudo-romantic school which simply tricks out a stereotyped adventure story in ruff and buskined hose, then sets a lot of bearded gentry to meaningless, if energetic, swashbuckling. This might be good, clean escapism, but it certainly does nothing to make the sound of that different drum ring true for the young reader.

The form is a bastard one, bred from the union of bad history with inadequate writing; and as a children's writer with respect both for my craft and for my readers, I am concerned by this. As a Scottish writer, aware that my country's history is largely unfamiliar to those outwith her borders, I am further concerned by the fact of its being so often distorted by these pseudo-romantics—and to such an extent, also, that one need look no further for an example of their genre.

Bonnie Prince Charlie—super-romantic name, immediately conjuring visions of David Niven in a blond wig planting the standard at Glenfinnan, with bold Highland chiefs flocking to greet him there. From mountain and glen, they rally their men. (One must be careful—the style, like plague, is infectious.) Fanatic in loyalty to their bonnie Prince, the Highlands rise to the summons of the Fiery Cross; and, with so many frilled jabots and lace cuffs in evidence that the scenario looks all chiefs and no Indians (for which latter, read "clansmen"), the kilted hordes clash on Culloden field with the Hanoverian army.

Disaster, alas, awaits. (Vignette of Charles on a white horse, looking anxiously bonnie.) The battle lost—in spite of much cantering back and forth on the white horse—Charles is forced to flee. He becomes "the Prince in the heather," a fugitive with thirty thousand pounds on his head, sheltered by motherly old ladies and beautiful young ones, with a last rearguard of frilled jabots and lace cuffs standing by to fight off pursuing dragoons.

No-one, not even for this king's ransom, can be found to betray him; and sorrowfully at last, he boards a ship for his return to France. Exit Charlie, to sad strains of pibroch lamenting, "Will ye no' come back again." Yet still, in lowly cottages as much as in fine mansions, the loyal toast to "the King over the water" is drunk, and Bonnie Prince Charlie remains forever enshrined in the hearts of the Scottish people.

Thus, the myth; but now for a cold, hard look at reality.

By the time Charles planted the standard in 1745, Scotland was sick of the Stuarts and their dynastic quarrels with the House of Hanover. The Lowlands wanted no part at all in this latest rebellion. In the Highlands, some clans were actively hostile to Charles, and showed this by fighting fiercely against him at Culloden. A majority of Highlanders were either indifferent to him, or only vaguely sympathetic. Only a few clan chiefs were actively loyal; and reluctantly, realising the odds against them, these few brought out their men. Still others hedged their bets, sending sons to fight for both sides, so that the family lands would be safe, whatever the outcome.

The clansmen who were summoned came reluctantly also to the Stuart standard—never at any time more than one in five of the available fighting men of the Highlands. By the April of 1746, when Culloden was fought, this had been reduced to one in eight, which number included hundreds forced to come out for Charles under threat of their homes burned and goods destroyed. The clan system was dying but not yet dead, and where a chief could not exact obedience by virtue of being father of his clan, he could still rule by fear.

The men thus forced out to Culloden field were the "humblies"—the lowest rank of a clan, naked of thigh and arm, their only weapon a broadsword. As the clan system demanded also, their sons—boys of fourteen in some cases—stood by them. Yet still, despite the reluctant loyalty of some in the Prince's army and the fearful obedience of others, every man there fought with a pertinacious ferocity that had them charging into the mouths of the English cannon even after their dead lay piled breast high to the charge. And from every man there, once the weak and indecisive generalship of Charles had lost them the day and he himself was cowardly fleeing the battlefield, a terrible price was exacted.

The dead from these charges were the lucky ones. The wounded suffered death by savage mutilation, or from exposure, with their women kept forcibly from rescuing them. Hanging and transportation for life were the most merciful of various horrible fates for all those taken prisoner. The men who escaped to their homes did so only to see their babies' brains bashed out, their women raped, their homes burned, stock and crops looted, the death penalty exacted for wearing the tartans which were their only clothing. And in all this, those who had not been "out" in the rebellion suffered equally with those who had; government policy now being to subdue the Highlands for ever by totally destroying the life of its people.

As for the so-called loyalty that would endure all this rather than betray the Bonnie Prince, his continued safety owed more to accident than to design. Honour played its part, of course, among those actively loyal to him. But for the rest, thirty thousand pounds was just too enormous a sum to be realised by men whose only income was a few pounds a year. Thirty pence—enough to feed a starving family for a week—would have been more temptation. Nor did the Highlands lack for spies, or for those who hated sufficiently to betray without reward; but the capture of Charles would not have put an end, in any case, to the cruelty of those "killing times," so that most Highlanders reserved their even greater hatred for his enemies.

And so once again, exit Charlie, with no pibroch this time except the cries of the dying, the screams of the terrified, the moans of the hungry; no comfort except his predilection for the bottle that was eventually to make him an alcoholic nuisance to everybody. He wasn't even bonnie, then or ever, poor lad —not with a receding chin, too large a nose, and a bad case of facial acne. The good looks were just another part of the myth, which itself was born thirty years later among the genteel ladies of Edinburgh, sipping tea in High Street drawing-rooms and achieving a vicarious thrill from composing the ubiquitous "Will ye no' come back again" and other Jacobite ballads.

There was no singing in the glens—only a grim endurance of want and persecution. This was what Culloden finally meant to the Highlands. But if the myth of the bonnie prince is to be destroyed in favour of reality, what happens to romance, to adventure? Are there to be no figures larger than life, no heroes of Culloden? Is there to be no laughter, no high moment of glory, no voice calling bravely out of the past to the youngster of the present day?

This is where truth scores, for true history blazes with moments no human imagination could invent; and topping them all at Culloden was that charge of the clans—the last charge in the last battle they were ever to fight on the soil of their own land. It was the only kind of fighting the clans knew, that charge; but professional soldiers everywhere spoke of it with awe, for it was more—much more—than a military tactic.

It was the visible, living history of the clan system, led by chiefs, officered by the sons of chiefs, clansmen surging behind in a great, powering wave, with pipes screaming the clan's war rant, every voice roaring the clan's war cry. It was pride of blood in action, men of one name all knit in a blind ferocity of courage to project a moment's glory on that name before they died.

This was why those forced men, those humblies and other reluctant supporters fought as they did at Culloden. And this was also why Murdoch McLeod, a fifteen-year-old pupil at Inverness Academy, played hookey from school that day, stole a broadsword, and was last seen on the battlefield enquiring for the men of McLeod so that he might stand by them.

Did young Murdoch also die under the English cannon? Or did he live to be punished for hookeying out of school, for that stolen sword, and borrowed dreams of glory? There is a tale here, and one voice at least that may call bravely from the past to any youngster, anywhere.

From Glenmoriston too, comes a ringing echo of the romance and high adventure that arose from even this sad shambles of dynastic war; and from a cave high up in the mountains there springs the true, yet still larger than life story of other heroes of Culloden—seven of them, to this very day still known as the Seven Men of Glenmoriston.

They had followed their chief to the battle, these seven. They were all young, all mountain men agile as deer, all reckless. They turned outlaw, refusing to surrender their arms on promise of the false pardon that led only to the gallows; and high up in their cave refuge in Corrie Dho, they led the existence of seven wild and merry Robin Hoods.

They drank wine stolen from under the very nose of the English commander at Fort Augustus. They plundered baggage trains of grain stolen from poor crofters, and gave it back to their own starving folk. Cunningly, when pursued, they directed their musket fire to make the maximum noise of ricochet from the mountains, and so created the impression of a small army concealed there. They had a leader who outdid them all in feats of daring; but for all their gay impudence, they had a short way with spies. Ruthlessly they dirked one of these to death, then stuck his severed head high on a tree as a warning to others; and it was this same bold Seven who eventually did get Charles away to France.

When all other means in this had failed, his friends

brought him to the Seven, and for the next six weeks he lived as one of their band. He called them his Privy Council, answered only to the Gaelic name they gave him, became their camp cook, and tried to teach them also to cook. He talked with the Seven, dreamed and laughed with them, adventured with them, for he was not at all a bad fellow, this young Charles; and to be a man among men at last seemed to give him—temporarily, at least—the grip on reality he had never before managed to achieve.

So at last also, in the cave in Corrie Dho, the dreams and reality of that Jacobite rebellion are transmuted into a tale that does not flinch from admitting the suffering of the times, salutes the high drama these brought forth, and bounds along with the youthful zest and elation of the seven young men themselves.

This is the very stuff of the historical novel. This is what is needed to create a book which can not only stand alone on its merits *as* a book, but which will also recreate some part of the past as a living link in the chain of human experience. Nor will anything less than this satisfy the definition of what an historical novel should be, for nothing less will make the sound of that different drum ring true for present-day readers; and with all the materials of history to hand, the only question that remains is how to use these to create such a book.

There are no limits of choice for the writer, in this; no barriers in terms of the time or country in which the book may be set, or the historical situation on which it may be based. None of these is relevant except insofar as it serves the main function of the source material—which is to yield a theme that has universal application and appeal. But for the realisation of this theme and its structuring into a novel, there are two essential requisites.

The first is inborn, and by no means peculiar to the writer. It has curiosity about the past in it, a feeling of the continuing significance of the past; but in sum, it is that indefinable quality, a sense of history. So much the better, also, if the writer is born into an environment which feeds this sense of history—and here, at least, I can speak with the certainty of having experienced this good fortune, for all my childhood impressions are of current time springing naturally from a still-living past.

The village smithy, where I had watched the forging of that wheel-rim, had fascinated a dozen generations of children before me. In some small fields of the farms around the village there was still seed broadcast by hand; and still, when it came to harvest, the curved rise and fall of shining sickle-blades, the ancient rite of shaping the last sheaf into a corn dolly to perch high on the stacked straw and thereby protect it from unnameable pagan fears of harm.

The shadow of history fell over me every day from the tree that had shaded George Wishart preaching the Reformation while John Knox carried a sword before him. Its shape filled my vision with castle, keep, and cottage, with barn, mill, and dovecote—or "dookit" as we called this last, in the native Doric speech which itself has the whole of Scotland's past in its sound and structure.

All this was my dear heritage; but instinctual appreciation of the past is not enough for the historical writer. Knowledge, a detailed yet embracing knowledge of the chosen source material is the second requisite essential to the craft. Yet for the writer, as distinct from the historian, this knowledge must also be free-ranging enough to light on the unexpected, the curious, the unique detail that may suddenly focus understanding more sharply than any number of vast and scholarly tomes.

Imagination springs freely from such moments of discovery. They are the philosopher's stone that instantly transmutes the leaden dross of history into story-gold; but the lines of formal study can be a bar to finding this talisman, and it was my further fortune never to be so restrained. Growing up in the depression days of the Hungry Thirties meant being too poor to have more than the legal minimum of formal schooling. Resentment at this drove me to libraries; and not knowing whom to trust among the many of all the authorities I read, drove me back to the original sources of history.

From State Papers, diaries, letters, inventories, legal records, I drew my own conclusions and carefully tested them against received wisdom. Nor did marriage and bringing up babies put a stop to this intensity of research, since I found it quite practicable—pleasurable also—to nurse a child in one arm and the current volume of study in the other. And gradually, from resenting the fact of never having had what I thought of as "a proper education," I turned to appreciating what this had meant to me as a writer.

The knowledge I had gained was academically sound—I had proved that. But no-one had ever conditioned my thinking on what I had learned. I had always been free to strike off on paths that made no difference to the main pattern of history; small, hidden paths that were no more than the tracks between village and village, between one person's house and another. I had peered in at windows, stood behind a housewife writing up her accounts, set off for school with a candle in my hand and a slate under my arm, run in terror along a dark city street when the watch had noticed me abroad after the curfew hour had struck.

I had discovered what it was to think, talk, eat, sleep, wake, in times other than my own; to work, worry, celebrate, mourn, as the people of those times had done, living among them, feeling with them, even dying as one of them—for I, too, had charged those guns at Culloden. I knew the whole pattern into which their lives had fitted, yet I also knew that more important thing which is what really makes the total pattern of history in the end—the quality of those lives. And simply because no-one had ever restrained the play of my imagination, I was free to recreate them in any way I willed.

This, for the historical novelist, must always be the end-purpose of research; to be able to think and feel in terms of a period so that the people within it are real and three-dimensional, close enough to hear the sound of their voices, to feel their body-warmth, to see the expression in their eyes. All the rest one learns—dates of events, types of weapon, location of incidents, political background—all the logistics of history, as it were, are no more than fixed points of reference for the structure of a book; and once the essential knowledge of them has been gained, they are simply something to be absorbed into the general pattern of one's practical awareness, to be used later in exactly the manner and only to the same degree as one would use knowledge of modern times in a book on contemporary life. They can influence plot, but they can never dictate it.

This is not a contradiction in terms, even although the plot of an historical novel revolves, by definition, around some factual event in the past. It was W. Somerset Maugham who said that a writer never thinks of a character in a vacuum, but always as doing something; and George Bernard Shaw who said that it was his characters and not himself who took charge of his plots. Both observations are true for any kind of writing, and the structuring of an historical novel is rather like using the ideas they contain to complete a jigsaw puzzle with half of its pieces missing.

One has a series of actual events, sometimes clearly related, sometimes apparently random within a certain space of time or setting. One has historical characters, well-known or otherwise, and all these form the available pieces of the jigsaw. The missing pieces are the fictitious characters—the people always mill-ing around in one's head "doing something." The shape and colouring of these pieces depends on what sort of people they are, and on this also depends their time, and method of slotting themselves into the jigsaw puzzle.

Where the writer has control in shaping the final picture is in deciding the point of entry into the story it will portray; but this is also the prime technical problem of any book, and never more so than in one drawn from a past unfamiliar to the young reader. Period and setting have to be established, and where adults are concerned, one can at least presume the modicum of knowledge which permits this to emerge from the developing text. No such presumption can be made for children; and so for them, the writer is additionally faced with casting his opening in a form that will convey the story's period and setting clearly, simply, and without apparent contrivance, at the same time as it sweeps them into its action.

This latter, finally, can only ever be one person's fictionalised concept of events which can never be truly known in their entirety; but so long as it subscribes to its own terms of reference—that is, a seemingly-natural synthesis of the known with the fictitious, through characters true to their period and reacting truly to their imagined natures—that concept is a valid one. Nor is the construction of it so mechanical as it may sound from this analysis—quite the reverse, in fact.

As in every inventive process, it takes moments of

inspirational clarity to relate theory to fact; and in structuring a book of this kind it may call for wild leaps of the imagination to take the scattered clues that history provides and build them into the needed complexity of richly-coloured plot and sub-plot. Yet without the technique to deploy it in this way, the writer's imagination remains an aimless force. Without an iron grasp on technique, there can be no risking of those leaps in imagination. Technique moulds, harnesses, governs. To recognise this fact is the first step in creating a book. To apply it is to provide every succeeding step with the power and direction essential to the whole.

As technique governs, so also must truth restrain. Research to the nth degree is the historical novelist's duty as well as pleasure, and it is only when evidence one way or another is finally lacking that the free play of imagination is permissible as well as necessary. The one thing that is *never* permissible is to distort any part of evidence, either by suppressing it to suit the story, or by tilting it to the balance of the writer's prejudice.

This is bad enough directed at adults, who can be assumed able to check the result at source, but children have no such safeguard. Where they are concerned, doctored truth is as bad as outright lies, and lying about history to children does more than take advantage of the inculcated respect that inspires trust in the printed word. It outrages their *right* to the truth.

History is. History is people's lives. The child reading the historical novel is also part of history, and to tamper with the known facts is to mock both those lives and the reader's apprehension of what they meant.

There can be challenges to this, of course; as, for instance—how can one truly present women in history without perpetuating the convention of the subject role? No single answer offers itself here; and certainly there is none to be found in the current idiocy which assumes rewriting to be a solution to the same dilemma in a related field—that of traditional tales for children.

Such tales, it has to be accepted, are simply a faithful reflection of one-time factual situations; and facts, as my own hard-headed countrymen would put it, are "chiels that winna ding." In effect, no amount of wishful thinking can alter facts; and the writer, in any case, is not a propagandist. But accepting facts still does not mean that one is slavishly bound by their implications. There is still nothing to prevent the writer selecting from historical situations that permitted some women fully to realise themselves as people, and—by contrast with an opposite situation—demonstrating the waste of potential that was the common lot.

A much more serious challenge could spring from the fact that some of the customs of a past day were utterly barbaric by present-day standards, and some of the most exciting sources of story are also the most violent of episodes in history. How does one truly present these to the young reader? How, for example, could one detail an incident involving an execution, the victim of which had been sentenced to be "chained prostrate on a hurdle, dragged to the place of execution, and there half-hanged, disembowelled, castrated, beheaded, and quartered."

This barbarity was first practised in England in the year 1305, and for five centuries thereafter, remained that country's sentence of execution on a traitor. Nothing so revolting has ever been known in Scotland, but it is still no hypothetical question for a Scot to ask how one may write about it, for this was the manner of death hatefully devised by Edward I of England to vent his spleen against a Scot, William Wallace. And Wallace was not only among the greatest of Scottish patriots. He was also that marvellous phenomenon of the human race, an ordinary man who rose to greatness through cherishing the idea of liberty; a freedom fighter who so powerfully forged the resistance of a nation that his stature dwarfs, by comparison, any modern claimant to the title.

In all the long, dark years of struggle against English attempts to enslave the Scottish nation, this idea of liberty was his one bright candle. With his last tortured breath he refused to admit the jurisdiction of the English king over him or over Scotland; and so, with that last breath also, he guarded the continuing right of the Scottish people to that same tiny flame.

Far from debasing him then, with this brutal death, Edward succeeded only in ennobling him. Wallace—Patriotism—Liberty. The names have ever since been synonymous in Scottish minds, and no author of any race could write of Wallace's life without telling also the manner of his death. No Scottish author who took liberty as a theme in writing for children could ignore Wallace as the hero of such a tale, and thus be faced also with the task of showing the martyrdom that made him even greater in death than in life.

The reading of such a finale, one might think, would be enough to make the most hardened adult shudder. And yet I recall reading many times as a child of those who suffered "a traitor's death," and feeling intense frustration at not knowing exactly what this phrase implied. I recall further, that even although I was horrified when I finally discovered the truth of it, I was also relieved to be rid of the pictures my own imagination had painted.

Scenes of blood and violence, in fact, are often a necessary part of externalising childhood's inner fears, and to project these scenes in context is totally different from gratuitously inserting them for effect. Shock—total, unrelated shock—is the effect of seeing a stranger brutally killed before one's eyes. To witness one's brother similarly murdered is to feel concern as well as horror, so that the shock is not only altered in character but diffused into a wider spectrum of sensation. In writing terms, this means aiming to so involve the reader with one's characters that either his sympathy is engaged or his hostility is satisfied when one or other of them is the victim of violence. So the reader eventually experiences catharsis—that purging of the emotions which is the useful function of violence in life; and as in life, so it should be in literature.

Horses for courses, as they say, and the methods of achieving this reader involvement are as various as the writer's technique will allow. But characterisation in depth is still necessarily the key to engaging the reader's emotions in depth; and—as in other forms of writing—characterisation is achieved primarily through the image projected in dialogue. Unfortunately, however, the dialogue of an historical novel is often the rock responsible for many a stumble.

"I'll believe that when I see it," said he, gives the immediate impression that "he" is a sceptical person, and this note of scepticism can be emphasised by restructuring the dialogue to read, *"I'll believe that,"* said he, *"when I see it!"*

A subsidiary use of dialogue—that of carrying action forward—could be served by making this read, *"I'll believe that,"* said he, seating himself, *"when I see it!"* Further extended, this scrap of dialogue serves yet another use—that of scene-setting; and, at the same time, deepens the characterisation to show confidence as well as scepticism.

"I'll believe that," said he, seating himself on the room's only chair, *"when I see it!"*

Beyond all these functions of dialogue, the historical novelist must also manage to convey the impression of speech forms common to past times, and this is where one may encounter archaisms scattered through a text like sprigs of parsley decorating a dish that otherwise tastes of anything but parsley. The opposite error is to attempt an academically accurate reproduction of dated speech forms, which—as well as being a check to smooth reading and therefore a stumbling-block to understanding—are incapable of serving the modern writer's threefold use of dialogue.

The dialogue the historical novelist must always settle for, in fact, is a clear, plain English which in itself is timeless, and which should be touched by the fashions of an age only where these can extend its main function. Rather than use the modern word "exceedingly," for instance, it would be correct in eighteenth-century terms to say "exceeding"; and the use of this obsolete form could characterise the typically conservative speech of a lawyer of that time remarking that his client was "an exceeding rich man."

For preference, of course, I would make this gentleman an Edinburgh lawyer, and so exercise the advantage enjoyed by any writer with access to a rich vein of native expression which not only answers to the criterion of timelessness, but also has qualities of originality and wit denied to that clear, plain English.

He's that mean, if he was a ghost he wouldn't give you a fright.

Thus the Scots way of describing a very miserly person, and salty comment like this is typical of shrewd observation in any age. Nothing could sharpen the clarity of its characterisation. No-one could better its brevity; and in narrative sequence also, these latter qualities should rule. Narrative carries the action scenes which give the story its forward impetus, and to write sharp, clear narrative is to achieve sharp, clear action. Brevity ensures fast action; and where dialogue occurs intermittently in an action sequence is where all the points already made apply most strongly. "Have a care!" may be strictly in period as a shout of warning. The timeless alarm which is sharper, clearer, and therefore most effective, is still, "Look out!"

Writing in narrative terms, also, one must always keep in mind the other burden they carry—which is reaction; in effect, the attitude of the story's characters to the events and ideas of their particular age. For a person to react untypically to these would normally be for him to step out of belief as a character within that age; but where the attitudes contemporary to this are not acceptable to the modern reader, the writer may not be able to gain the sympathy he needs for such a character without making him untypical.

A bald statement to this effect achieves no more than making him seem a modern in fancy dress—like that consistently-recurring historical hero who baths and grooms himself every day in an age where bathing was so rare that everyone wore body odour like a second skin, and hair-combing so infrequent that lice were permanent residents. The man within that sweet-smelling skin will inevitably be a modern in mental as well as physical attitudes, and thus quite unbelievable in context of his own time.

To be specific on this as it might occur in a story for

children, one could suitably take a situation in which children have a very positive interest—that of breaking-up for the school holidays. And to back-project on this, one might instance the ritual anciently marking the end of the Easter term in the parish schools of Scotland—a main, or series of contests, between game-cocks.

Every boy in school brought a trained bird to fight in this event. The centre of the classroom was the cockpit. The members of the Town Council sat around as honoured guests. The schoolmaster presided over the play—which was a knockout competition leaving only one bird surviving—and at the end of the various rounds claimed all the dead birds as a perquisite for his Easter dinner.

The cruelty of cockfighting has long been recognised, and the bloody shambles of birds pecked and spurred to death at such a main must have been truly horrifying. But the boys setting those birds on to one another certainly did not recognise this as cruelty. Neither did the dominie who taught them, nor yet the Town Councillors kindly lending their patronage. Only a flash of insight such as occasionally informs our own unthinking acceptance of present-day cruelties could have given them such recognition. And this is the writer's problem—how to present that cockfight as the glorious celebration it was for these schoolboys, at the same time as he provides at least one character in the scene with the insight to realise the cruelty involved.

A wounded bird fighting with gallantry against

odds might focus insight for this character, especially if the creature had been a favourite, carefully nurtured. This is the least difficult part of the problem—finding the situation which will solve it. Much more difficult is the technical development of that situation—a matter which calls for the writer to project two differing attitudes; that of the careless enjoyment proper to the time of the story, and—through a character who must never be allowed to step outside the frame of reference provided by that time—the perception of cruelty proper to the writer's own time.

What the situation demands from him, in effect, is more than the division of personality that normally enables the writer to live in two sets of circumstances—his own, and that of his characters. The time factor that calls for him to relate two opposed thought patterns is the complication in that exercise —as it is in all the work of the historical novelist. And with this in mind, the answer to the problem must always finally rest in allowing the pattern of the past to *appear* to dominate, when what takes place in reality is a channelling of this through the thought patterns of the writer's own time.

So the feelings behind the pattern of that past time can also be recreated for the reader; feelings he will then discover are essentially the same as his own. Out of this, faces will emerge; the faces of people he will recognise to be simply reflections of himself. And out of the knowledge of these people's experience will come some idea of the bald truth in Housman's words:

The troubles of our proud and angry dust,
Are from eternity, and cannot fail.
Bear them we can; and if we can, we must. . . .

But this is far from the end of it, for the child learning to relate himself and his own time to the life and times of all those figures from the past, is doing so to the beat of that different drum; and there is more than tragedy in its tumult. There is also the grim gaiety of Housman's last line—"Shoulder the sky, my lad, and drink your ale." And in this, is the final extent of the kinship the young reader of the historical novel may find, for only humans are thus capable of jesting with fate.

Other forms of the animal creation may court danger, but only humans swagger in the face of fear, make a mental theatre of threat, pursuit, capture, escape, endeavour, contest, or discovery. Only humans seek adventure for adventure's sake, and boast—as in G.K. Chesterton's lines—the very attraction of its perils:

How white their steel, how bright their eyes,
I love each laughing knave!
Cry high, and bid him welcome,
To the banquet of the brave. . . .

Only humans greet death like this—with a laugh, a flourish; with panache! And unless or until something happens to interfere seriously with human nature, this will always be so.

The child bent over the book is of the same breed—

born to shoulder the sky, yet still having deep within him that quality of panache and the need to identify with those who have gloriously expressed it. . . . Let the drum beat! Let it call him to that banquet of the brave—the company of his own kind through the ages. He will discover who he is in what they were; and through wandering with them, will truly come home at last.

One
World

"There's a ghost in Baker's Wood," said my sister. And we said—half wanting to believe her and half afraid to—

"Go on, there isn't! You're making that up."

"No, I'm not. It's the ghost of a baker that hanged himself. Why d'you think it's *called* Baker's Wood?"

None of us could think of an answer to that. Besides which, although she was only twelve years old, my sister was still the oldest child there—which made the rest of us pretty small fry. And of course, there was that bit in us that wanted to believe her. We fled past the darkness of Baker's Wood and fetched up half a mile away, still frightened, yet giggling with delight in ourselves. We'd tricked that old ghost, we had!

Everyone has some recollection of a similar childhood incident. Tucked away at the back of the mind perhaps, but still there, is some memory of the imagined terror that has such fascination for children; and many people must also have recall of one further experience common in childhood—the feeling that around any corner I might catch a sudden glimpse of something strange and wonderful. I remember vividly how I longed for this something with an oddly poignant yearning; and as a writer now, I find that the form of children's literature which best exemplifies both that fascinated terror and the yearning is what—for lack of a more exact name—we refer to as fantasy.

The title is inexact, of course, because this is such a wide-ranging genre, covering everything from Snow White and the Seven Dwarfs to the adventures of astronauts in future time. But the basis of all such tales is the same. Their ingredients have a common source in recurring elements of the tales from folklore with which we in the Western world are familiar. Moreover, all successful essays into fantasy have one result in common; and my purpose now is to examine the background to this result, and from this to assess its significance in children's literature.

A brief look at the technicalities of writing fantasy is a first necessary step in this, so many writers having tried the form and failed for lack of realising one simple truth. Fantasy is not simply absurdity piled upon absurdity until some climactic point is reached. However skilful the writer may be in handling such a situation, the initial credibility gap will still be too wide for the main outline of the story to be acceptable; and even if the reader perseveres in trying to bridge this gap, interest will fall away simply because the story contains no natural and easy means of identification with its characters.

True fantasy, on the other hand, is always firmly rooted in fact, or in some instantly-recognisable circumstance acceptable to the reader—even if this latter is itself fantastic. One may say, for instance, "There was a boy once made himself a whistle." Or: "The starship *Endeavour* took off for an unknown universe." The first is the factual type of opening which provides instant reader identification with a character. The second opening postulates a circumstance which in itself is fantasy, in the sense of being technically impossible; yet it is still so recognisably a projection from known facts that the reader can instantly associate with these, and thus once again identify.

In the case of the first type of opening, the writer's skill must be directed towards pursuing this reader-identification to the point where character and reader are mutually engaged in some experience involving creatures of fantasy. In the case of the second, the reader's initial acceptance of a fantastic circumstance is furthered by peopling it with "real"—i.e. human—characters, and then similarly achieving mutual involvement of characters and reader.

The "fantastic fact" story basis can, of course, be placed far back in time as well as far forward—as, for instance, "There was once a dwarf lived all alone in a dark forest"—an opening which postulates a circumstance so old in story terms that the reader's mind slides back in time as automatically as it jumps forward for a fantasy of the future. "Racial memory" or "ancestral memory" are the terms variously used to explain this easy reaching back to ancient thought patterns, and the phenomenon is one which is at least partly responsible for ready acceptance of all the folklore elements in fantasy. Paradoxically, also, one has only to glance at the most apparently modern of fantasies—the starship odyssey—to see immediately how some of these elements occur.

The Captain of this starship is always an identifiably human person; but always also he is its ultimate authority figure, and thus the folklore equivalent of "the king of that country." Who, then, is the creature who stands at his elbow advising him—the being who hails from a planet other than earth and is gifted with "paranormal" powers? One of his "interplanetary" crew, of course—but also the folklore equivalent of the court magician.

The starship is threatened by the inhabitants of another planet—a race possessing an inexplicably advanced technology. In folklore terms, the king finds he has to counter magic. Lieutenant Magician, however, is able to explain that all the power of this technology is controlled by a device worn by the alien ruler—in folklore terms, the ring or amulet which is commonly pictured as conferring magic power. To capture the device therefore becomes the Captain's aim. But alas, possession of this is guarded by the impenetrable casket in which this ruling

60

figure sleeps—parallels again, in the thicket around Sleeping Beauty, the glass case around Snow White; or else it is hidden in some complex of underground caves—a parallel with innumerable folktales of dwarfs guarding treasure deep in the mine under a magic mountain. . . . And so the story proceeds, taking a little bit here from this tradition of folklore, a little bit there from that; and proving in the process that Ecclesiastes was right in saying, "There is no new thing under the sun"—not even the adventures of a starship!

Further support than this is needed, however, for the claim that all fantasy is rooted in folklore, and the support comes first of all from defining the word "folklore" itself. The key to this definition is in "lore," which is derived from an Old English root interpreted as meaning either the act of teaching, or that which is learned. Thus folklore is what people have learned and passed on through the ages—in effect, the traditions, beliefs, customs, sayings, stories, superstitions, and prejudices preserved by word of mouth among the common people; and even where no oral chain of communication existed, within their racial or ancestral memory.

A very long stretch of time is implied in this definition; in the case of the stories which embody most other aspects of folklore, a much longer period than illustrators of the first recorded versions would have us suppose. Indeed, to find the origins of such tales, we must go as far back as the first imaginative uses of speech, for folktales are not a spontaneous act of invention. Far from this, they are the result of diverse experience over a long period in a wide variety of settings, with imagination only very gradually shaping the accreted knowledge of this experience into story form. With justice, in fact, they might well be called a people's record of events dating from prehistoric times—as perhaps one example could serve to demonstrate.

In the Orkney Islands, to the north of Britain, there is a structure known as Maes Howe. A "howe" in Orkney dialect is a hill, and Maes Howe from the exterior does present the appearance of a rounded, grass-covered hill. Its interior, however, shows it to be a megalithic monument of unique grandeur, a stone tumulus constructed with superb precision to be the burial hall of priests, or kings. For more than thirty centuries Maes Howe has dominated the Orkney plain on which it stands, and—in the words of the late Eric Linklater—it shows that the men who built it had "a working knowledge of mathematics, a priest-king to whose teaching they listened, and immortal longings."

Thirty centuries ago, on a tiny windswept island in the wild waters of the North Sea? Who could have visualised the existence of such a people, or such an achievement in building? And when the grass grew over the outer walls of Maes Howe, who could have believed the story of the great hall it concealed?

No-one did, in fact; no-one except the humble fishermen and farmers of that same island. It was they, century after century after century, who preserved the tale of Maes Howe as an artificial structure instead of the natural hill it seemed to be; and such was the strength of this legend that other men eventually heeded it. A party of twelfth-century Viking warriors broke through the roof of this strange tomb to plunder the treasure of its buried priest-kings. They left a record of their exploit in runes carved on the interior of its stone walls; and in their turn, they too were absorbed into the folktale of Maes Howe. But still it remained only a folktale, despised as a source of accurate information about the past; until late in the nineteenth century when the resurgence of interest in folklore caused heart-searching among at least some of the learned people who had previously been so contemptuous. Maes Howe was among the phenomena investigated during this period, and the truth so long preserved in the folktale was finally proved.

The mind conditioned to accept rapidly-changing patterns of culture finds it difficult, of course, to appreciate just how slowly all such tales have accreted; difficult also to grasp how very gradually imagination has transmuted the long experience they span, and how folk memory alone has transmitted them. In yet another group of these northerly islands, however, there is most striking evidence of the circumstances that made all this process possible—physical evidence in the shape of a small area of settlement continuously occupied for more than three thousand years, from the Stone Age onwards.

Jarlshof is the name of this settlement. It lies on

one of the Shetland Islands, and the site it occupies is a complex of building remains which show houses of the Bronze Age constructed among and around and on top of the earlier Stone Age dwellings. A wheelhouse and a broch of the Iron Age are planted squarely among the Bronze Age ruins. The ninth-century farmhouses of Norse settlers stand cheek by jowl with those buildings of pre-history. Later buildings by thirteenth-century Norsemen have been supplanted by a mediaeval farmstead; and towering over all these remains are the high, broken walls of a sixteenth-century mansion.

A great variety of artefacts and other physical evidence of occupation has been uncovered in these ruins, and much of it goes to show that the different cultures involved were not only contiguous, but widely overlapping—stone tools continuing to be used well into the era of bronze, and bronze weapons until late after the working of iron was well established, with household utensils, food, and methods of cultivation all showing similar degrees of overlapping.

Jarlshof, in fact, is an excellent demonstration of the fact that social development in past time was not the stratified process into which it has been simplified by modes of thought prevailing in the nineteenth and early twentieth centuries; and where there has been an intermingling of physical cultures, there must inevitably also have been intermingling of all those component parts which go to make up the definition of folklore.

This is where we see the chain of communication through the centuries—the long, unbroken line of folk memory stretching in the case of Maes Howe from Megalithic times to the present day, and channelled enroute by those Norse raiders seeking plunder in the tomb of legendary priest-kings. This is where we begin to see the reality behind the fantastic facade of the tale, and to sense how the tale itself has grown from the interweaving of events and situations known to one age, only dimly remembered by ages following, and embellished by the imagination of later ages. This, finally, is where we should begin to appreciate that no such thing as pure fantasy exists. There is only a succession of folk memories filtered through the storyteller's imagination, and since all mankind shares in these memories, they are the common store on which the modern storyteller must draw in his attempts to create fantasy.

Closely related to this is my other stated contention on the technicalities of writing fantasy. A solid base of fact or apparent fact is required for the reader to be able to identify; and as an example of how this operates in folklore terms, I instance a type of tale which very clearly demonstrates how fantasy springs from the folktale mixture of the known, the remembered, and the imagined. There may be variation of detail in this type of story—which I always think of as "the Princess legend"—but the broad lines of it are always the same.

A kingdom is troubled by some great danger. The King tries every method to combat it, and fails. In despair, he offers the hand of his daughter and half his kingdom to the champion who will rid the kingdom of its danger. All the knights of the Court take up the challenge. All fail. All the brave men of the country also take the test, and fail. Finally, a challenger appears from outside the charmed circle of the brave and knightly—a poor boy from some unregarded corner of the kingdom, or from outside it altogether. He applies resourcefulness where blind courage has failed, wins the hand of the Princess and half the kingdom. And when the old King dies, poor boy and Princess reign in his stead over the whole kingdom and live happily ever after.

This, on the surface, is pure fantasy; but its charm is no more than a facade for certain stern facts of socio-political life in prehistoric Europe. For "kingdom" in this setting, one must read "tribal unit"; and for "King," the husband of the tribe's matriarch; for the situation embodied in the tale clearly points to a time when such tribal units managed to preserve identity and territorial rights through the system of matrilinear succession.

The idea behind this rule of succession was that a man cannot count on having sons who will rule wisely, but he *can* choose a son-in-law who will serve this purpose. Thus, succession to the ruling rights devolved through the eldest daughter of a line, with a husband carefully tested for more than his obvious qualities; and, to avoid consanguinity or internecine plotting, from as far beyond the Court circle as possible.

Rule over half the kingdom was the further sensible device adopted to induct this young man into a share of the chieftainship at the moment the physical authority of the matriarch's husband was reckoned to be passing its peak; the matriarch and her ageing husband gaining thereby from the authority of the young man's physical strength, the young couple by the advice of the older pair. And on the death of the older man, the young man achieved the full position he had won by marriage.

They lived happily ever after is the seal the storyteller finally sets on what started out as fact; and through a long, slow working of memory and imagination eventually took on the air of fantasy. Yet still it is a story which continues to *seem* grounded in fact, for this is the true art of the storyteller—to make his tale appear to relate to the lives of his hearers. The poor boy of the tale is no faceless character, but an anti-hero with whom we can laugh and sympathise. The champions who fail are part of the established privilege he topples. The Princess, perhaps, is the spoiled brat we would all like to see suitably tamed. All the initial elements in the tale have some comparable dimension in real life; and thus we start out with so firm a grip on seeming fact that we never notice the point where this takes off into fantasy, and carries us, soaring, with it.

This is a process that applies even to the furthest realm of fantasy—the supernatural. Yet once again, there is often writing which strives so hard for effect that it fails altogether to place the supernatural truly in context in fantasy; and fails, accordingly, to reach the take-off point that carries the imagination of the reader soaring effortlessly into that furthest realm. And so once again also, we need an objective look at folklore—this time to define the significance of the role played in it by the supernatural.

A contradiction in terms immediately presents itself here, for some aspects of the supernatural in folklore can clearly be seen to be founded also in fact; and so an initial step in this must be to divide all these aspects into two broad categories, the first one taking in creatures and objects which were themselves natural but which were thought to have supernatural powers.

The barrel of meal which never ran done, for instance, is an obvious example of wish-fulfilment. And just as obviously, the frequent tales of the stranger hero who appears riding a horse which runs faster than the March wind, point to a time when the horse was a previously-unknown and therefore impressive phenomenon to certain primitive peoples. Thus far one can go with the aid of deductive reasoning; but research can take us even further in examining this category of the supernatural, and here I would particularly instance the seal legends common in the north of Scotland and the islands of Orkney and Shetland.

Here are the great breeding grounds of the grey Atlantic seal, and all these legends concern this creature's supernatural power to shed its skin and take human form. In this way, it was said, seals could come ashore to marry, and even interbreed with humans—as happened on one occasion when a young Shetland fisherman was walking late on a moonlit night by a lonely beach.

Suddenly he heard music—girls' voices singing on a strangely high and sweet note. The next moment he saw the girls. They were dancing, and singing as they danced. Their hair flowed free. Their bodies were white and supple in the white moonlight. Enchanted, the young man hid behind a rock to watch them, and close to his hand discovered a pile of sealskins. Instantly then, he understood the meaning of the scene, and determined to have one of those beautiful girls for his own. Snatching up a skin, he made off with it, and all the other seal-women immediately ran to recover their skins and plunge back into the sea.

The girl whose skin he had stolen was helpless to do this. Without the skin she could not assume her seal form again, and so she followed him, begging and pleading to have it returned. But the young man was adamant. Marriage to this particular beauty was what he planned, and seeing no help for it, the girl agreed to become his wife.

The couple had two children—two boys, who could not understand why their mother searched everywhere in the house whenever their father was away at sea, and wept as she searched.

"What are you looking for, Mammy?" they kept asking. And always she answered them,

"Nothing you would understand. Nothing you would understand."

The younger of the two boys was not satisfied by

this. Still he persisted with his questions, and driven beyond endurance by this at last, the mother told him,

"It's just an old sealskin your Daddy's hidden somewhere. That's what I need to find."

The boy had the sharp eyes of childhood, and long ago he had discovered where his father had hidden the stolen skin.

"Is that all?" said he, and led his mother to the hiding-place.

The mother seized the skin, recognised it for her own, and hurried back to the sea with it to take her seal form again—although, the story most touchingly ends, "she grat sore to leave the bairns." That is, "she wept bitterly to leave the children."

There is an odd little ring of truth in this last, moving detail. Indeed, for all the fantasy of the concept behind it, the whole story is an interestingly circumstantial one, and research has indicated a primitive source in contacts that once existed between the natives of Shetland and other islanders they referred to as "Finns." They came from an island-group lying off the Norwegian port of Bergen, these Finns, and were known to use tiny canoes of sealskin, which they handled most skilfully. This gave them the power to exact a sort of tribute from the fishermen of Shetland, and the legends of Shetland portray these Finns as magicians, with the sealskin boats as their true skins. Robbed of these skins, therefore, their magic was rendered harmless. Lacking them, they could not escape back to the sea; and so there seems little doubt that this kind of story also rests very solidly on factual circumstance ignorantly perceived, and imaginatively interpreted.

To turn now to the second category of the supernatural in folklore is to consider those creatures whose form and substance is only apparent, in the sense that they are simply manifestations of a world which itself has no physical existence. Chief among these, it is generally thought, are the fairies of folklore, but fairies are not so easily categorised. Some theorists see strong affinities between our familiar fairylore and a much wider-ranging body of tales rooted in the religious influences of prehistoric times. Anthropologists, on the other hand, instance this familiar material as an example of folk memory preserving a strong tradition of the small-statured tribes which once inhabited northern and western Europe.

My own feeling is that fairylore owes something to each of these sources—a theory I have dealt with at suitable length on pages 81–95 of "The Otherworld"; but for the time being at least, it can be said that fairies do not conclusively come within this second category. The beings which do properly belong to it, however, are both as varied and as truly insubstantial as the fears that bred them—the wraiths and fetches of Celtic legend, for instance, the hound of death, and all other apparitions of foreboding. One could further instance such concepts as earth godlings like the "gruagach" of the Scottish Highlands, which had to be given its libation of milk every day in case it would take the strength of the cows in the

dairy; the mischievous Puck of English legend—
which name in turn derives from the Slavic "*bog*"
through the Scots-Gaelic "boucca"—all of them
again meaning an earth-spirit: the closely-linked
"pooka" of Irish legend, which was a mischievous
spirit in animal form, the kelpie or water-horse of
Scottish legend, goblins, demons, and every other
kind of unearthly form. Yet all of these are still no
more than personalised manifestations of some fear
or longing, a projection of the imagination on a situation or setting which inspired emotion of some kind.

How these beings first entered into folklore is
something that would require a book in itself to examine, but perhaps the best illustration of how they
have persisted is in the Irish Puck Fair, at Killorglin,
in County Kerry—the "Pook" Fair, as it is pro-
nounced there; for here we can see the relationship
to the pooka in the "pook" (i.e. the "puck," or wild
mountain goat) which is captured for the occasion
and reigns for three days as King of the Puck Fair.

All sorts of stories are told to explain the origin of
this festival, which takes the form of a three-day orgy
of drinking, dancing in the streets, and a horse-sale
that brings tinkers and farmers from all over Ireland
flocking to Killorglin. But the people of that place
themselves admit that no-one really knows why or
when it all began, and only the atavism of the ritual
proceedings involved points to the truth.

The Puck is brought into the village with great
ceremony, riding on a cart filled with flowering
heather. Following this come other carts, carrying

72

young girls dressed in white and handing out bunches of heather to the waiting crowds. At the centre of the village is a platform, built sixty feet high for this occasion. The procession halts at its foot, one of the girls crowns the Puck with a golden crown, and a band plays while the other girls dance in his honour. The Puck is then hoisted on to the platform itself, and tethered there with food and water to last him for the three days he will reign over the Fair. And there he stays, high above all the horse-dealing and the dancing, the gipsies telling fortunes, the stalls selling hot crubeens, long eyes winking amber under his golden crown—an elemental creature at the heart of an elemental celebration.

Is he the pooka in visible, living form? One could reasonably guess that the intent originally was to show him so, but all one could truly say of him and his ilk is that man was very near the tap-root of his existence when such creatures were first visualised. His senses were all keener than they were ever to be again; his body was tuned to the pulse of life all around him, his mind sensitive to every emanation of thought and feeling. He was a fearful creature, with the imagination to invent danger even where none existed; a thinking creature who had to find some way to explain to himself all those curious sensations of mind and body. And so he was an animist, imputing a spirit of life to everything in his world—sun, grass, wind, water, tree, stone.

His imagination gave shapes and names to these hidden presences, forms without substance which

73

were yet as real to him as anything which could be seen or touched; and thus, by personalising his fears, he was able to define them. He invented a magic to counter the power he sensed in their unseen world; and thus he succeeded in controlling his fear of it, making this manageable even to the point where he could enjoy frightening himself with tales of the supernatural. And—perhaps—hold a Puck Fair!

A background of inherited thinking like this was inevitably a potent factor, too, in tales springing from events and situations in folk memory—especially since all these are rooted in times when magic continued to be commonly practised and was universally believed to be effective. The subjective viewpoint which accepted magic as an agency of any event or situation, the appetite for the marvellous which is no more than the old childhood longing to glimpse the strange and wonderful around every corner—these were the other ingredients of the thinking which automatically seized on the supernatural as an explanation of the otherwise inexplicable in folk memory —the horse that could run fast as the wind, the meal barrel that never became empty, the seal which turned into a beautiful young woman. . . . Time and the storytelling imagination did the rest, gradually achieving the apparent fantasy of the folktale from this wholly natural and therefore perfect and inevitable blend of fact and fancy.

Compare now the workings of this sort of mind with that of the modern child reading a fantasy drawn from these same sources.

The very early years of this child will also have been a totally animistic period, when spatial concepts were so incompletely grasped that objects could inexplicably leap out to hurt him, when favourite toys had names and therefore personalities which had fantasies of adventure woven around them; and when unseen, uncomprehended forces like a strong wind felt like the hand of some giant creature lifting him up. By his scale of measurement also, everything beyond his immediate surroundings belongs to a giant world, which is therefore full of menace for him. His physical senses are at their most acute, his emotions at their most perceptive. His delights are all in things which seem to have some magical significance —notice the face of a small child listening for the first time to the tick of a watch. His fears are the fears of the unknown, the inexplicable—watch the face of a small child seeing a storm for the first time.

In the first few years of life, in effect, the modern child undergoes a compressed form of all the physical, mental, and emotional experiences through which his primitive forebears developed; and when he reaches reading age, he has not entirely left this fantasy world behind him. Total memory of it will be dim, but the delights will stand out all the sharper for that. Language will have given him a point of reference for his fears, so that he will be able to control his memory of them—even to the point where they, too, take on the edge of delight which comes from knowing there is some ultimate safety from them. Becoming bolder with this knowledge, he will actually invent new terrors—as we did with the ghost in Baker's Wood—just for the sake of enjoying that dangerous edge of delight; and the further he grows from them in terms of years, the more he will be able to manipulate the balance of those fears and pleasures that engage his deepest nature.

Yet still there are forces within this growing child that urge him inexorably on towards the adult world of rational concepts, so that for some years of his growth, he is a divided personality. From the age of about eight, say, to around twelve years, one half of him longs to remain in his now-manageable fantasy world; the other half is eager to be accepted into the "real" world of adults, and the story which appears naturally to merge these two worlds in one can be his imaginative release.

This is the significance that fantasy has in children's literature, and this is the result that all successful essays into fantasy have in common. They integrate the real and the imagined world so closely into one wholly believable one that the child-reader is no longer conscious of any division in his own personality. For the time the story lasts, at least, there is no "pull devil, pull baker" between his inherited subjective feelings which accept magic and the supernatural, and the growth of his objective viewpoint which urges him to put aside those feelings.

The transition from one mode of thinking to the other will come eventually, of course; but in the child's good time when, by his own volition, he is wholly ready to accept it. Moreover, if the writer of fantasy has served him well enough, there will always be some talisman—a sight, a scent, a sound, a touch—which can take him back to this world where imagination and experience were so closely integrated—this perfect, one world of fantasy.

The return will be brief, of course, and the occasions of return will grow fewer over the years, but this is a natural progression and most people would not wish it otherwise. The world of reality, after all, has no room for wistful backward-looking; and even if it had, there are no more than a few people who actively retain the desire for something known in childhood, or have the capacity to evoke it at will. These few, moreover, soon become strangers to their fellows, for they are the incomprehensible ones—the dreamers who take the sky for their skull, the ribs of mountains for their bones; who sense always with the faculties of the primitive, and see always with the wondering eye of the child.

They are the ones who never pass a secret place in the woods without a stare of curiosity for the mystery implied in all its mounds and hollows; who still turn corners with a lift of expectation at the heart. And to be a writer of fantasy, one must be among those few—those fortunate few; for, to produce a work that answers to all the demands of fantasy is suddenly to turn the corner which does at last show something strange and wonderful waiting to be seen, and—most gloriously—to know that long-ago sense of yearning at last fulfilled.

The
Otherworld

A curious thing happened in Scotland in the year 1692; a matter which arose from the sudden death of a certain Mr. Robert Kirk, who was then minister of Aberfoyle, a village in the Highlands of Scotland.

Mr. Kirk had been a man of considerable scholarship, and he had not previously shown signs of ill health. More remarkably, he had also been a seventh son of a seventh son, and thus gifted with that ability which, in those parts, is termed "the second sight." His studies had included fairylore in all its aspects, and in the year before his death he had written a small treatise entitled *The Secret Commonwealth Of Elves, Fauns, And Fairies.*

Mr. Kirk had been a man of evident common sense, in spite of his occult powers, yet this work had been composed in all seriousness, and was intended as an exact study of the structure of this "Secret Commonwealth" and of the nature of its inhabitants. The circumstances of his death are therefore worth noting.

The cause of it was apparently some kind of seizure suffered while out walking near his own church, and the place where the seizure overcame him was the slope of what his Gaelic-speaking parishioners called a "sithbhruaich"—a fairy hill. His body was carried home from there, buried in Aberfoyle churchyard, and the curious thing which happened after that event was that Mr. Kirk—or some shape which appeared to be Mr. Kirk—made itself visible to a relative. The shape spoke, commanding its hearer to take a message to another man—a mutual relative named Grahame of Duchray; and the exact words of the command were these:

> Say to Grahame of Duchray, who is your cousin as well as my own, that I am not dead but a captive in Fairland; and only one chance remains for my liberation. When the posthumous child, of which my wife has been delivered since my disappearance, shall be brought to baptism, I shall appear in the room, when, if Duchray shall throw over my head the knife or dirk which he holds in his hand, I may be restored to society; but if this is neglected, I am lost for ever.

Mr. Kirk's "fetch," as such a manifestation is called in the Highlands, did appear at the baptism as promised, where—to quote the only surviving account of it—"it was visibly seen." But Duchray was so shaken by this apparition that he did not throw his dirk over its head. The apparition vanished, and neither Mr. Kirk nor his fetch was ever seen again. For well over a hundred years after that time, however, tradition in Aberfoyle persisted in claiming that the body buried in the churchyard there had been only an appearance of Mr. Kirk; that the grave, in fact, was empty, and that the real Mr. Kirk had indeed been taken captive by the fairies *because he knew too much about them*—and, of course, because he had been bold enough to commit that knowledge to paper in his treatise on "the Secret Commonwealth."

1692 may seem a surprisingly late date to find belief in fairies still so active a part of people's thinking—especially the thinking of such learned men as Mr. Kirk. Yet this is not so, once one has explored the origins of that considerable body of folklore which should be more specifically termed fairylore. Moreover, as a present-day writer of fairy tales, it seems to me that the psychology of belief in fairies, and even of the wish to believe in them, has important implications for adults as well as for children of modern times. And yet, no exploration of these implications is possible without first dismissing entirely our modern concept of the fairies themselves.

This latter appears to stem from ignorant and therefore literal interpretation of poetic fancy in early English literature; and the distortion has continued by way of coy Victorian nursery tales to achieve the ultimate parody of fairies as minute, gossamer-winged creatures, looking like animated insects with infant human faces of revolting procrocity, and behaving in a manner as grotesque as their features. Debased fantasies such as these are now of such common currency, however, that they have almost blotted out the original concept of fairies as it occurs in folklore; and this, in many ways, is a cruel mishandling of a unique heritage from an almost inconceivably ancient past.

The origins of fairylore are so remote, indeed, that any examination of them takes us right back to the three main cultural streams of pre-historic Europe—all of these apparently of Eastern origin, all of them carrying some influence from a basic religious belief termed "the Cult of the Dead." Death, in this belief, was only an appearance, not a reality. A world beyond the grave was thus evoked, named according to the specific culture which refined this idea, and peopled with the gods, the dead heroes, and the revered ancestors of that culture.

Thus also, we have the concept of Elysium, and of Valhalla, from the Graeco-Roman and Nordic-Teutonic cultures. From the third cultural stream—that of the Celtic nations—we have Avalon; or, to give it in the Scottish Gaelic which sprang from the common language of the Celts, Tir nan Og, the Land of Youth. All these concepts of a life beyond death have some connections with fairylore; but the translation of Tir nan Og is noteworthy, since—as will be shown—it implies a difference in belief from those other cultures. There is a further term for this shadow-land visualised in the Celtic culture—"the Otherworld"; and it is mainly from the Celtic folklore common to northern and western Europe that we have the great body of superstition which has given rise to fairy stories.

As one might expect, however, there are conflicting theories on the reasons for these superstitions. The metaphysical approach claims that they are rooted in the basic subscription to the belief behind the Cult of the Dead. Anthropologists claim that fairy stories enshrine a tradition of the very early inhabitants of northern and western Europe—nomadic and comparatively small-statured tribes dispersed gradually to outlying moor, hill, and bog by successive waves of immigrants of developing agricultural habit.

How much reliance to place on either theory can only be judged by looking at the differing forms of support it has from various sources—folklore, archaeological findings, the early pagan poetry and later Christian traditions of the Celts; also, the very much later legal records on those unfortunates accused of the crime which in Scotland was called "consorting with the Queen of Elphame"—i.e. the Fairy Queen—and which carried the death penalty. None of this evidence can be properly assessed, however, without first giving some clearer definition of the Celtic Otherworld, and noting how it differs from those other concepts of a land beyond death.

The Graeco-Roman culture had its dark and hateful Hades as a separate region of death and a counterpart to the happy Elysian Fields. Nordic culture had bleak and hunger-stricken Hel opposed to joyful Valhalla. Nearly all mythologies, in fact, speak of two separate places of reward and punishment after death; but the Celtic concept is a unified one which contains no hint of dark or infernal regions. "Good" and "bad" simply did not enter the Celts' thinking on such matters—indeed, all the evidence of their poetry, their art, their legend, shows them for a people who took such fierce and sensual joy in life that it would be only natural for them to visualise it as continuing beyond the grave in a way that heightened its pleasures. The Celtic land of the dead might therefore be more aptly termed the land of the living, for it was there also that heroes became even braver, fair women more than ever beautiful, and where laughter, feasting, and joyful war were all relished in perpetual youth.

The location of this land was vague, of course, since it was a purely subjective concept—"land over the waves," "land of heart's desire," and "the west" are other names for it in Celtic legend. Yet side by side with all his conjectures about this, the poetry of the Celt's imagination also enabled him to conceive of this immaterial orld as one which interpenetrated the material world of his five senses, was immanent in every aspect of it, yet still was transcendent to it. This is also how Celtic legend pictures the world of fairies; so that, in effect, it made no real distinction between the two.

The very poetry of the Celtic concept, however, is

something which makes it very difficult for us to tell how far imagination distinguished between this fairy, or Otherworld, and the region to which mankind in general went after death; but folklore preserves many tales of humans briefly permitted to visit the fairy world—usually to perform some menial office, such as nursing a fairy child—and in the course of this, glimpsing other humans long since dead yet still somehow translated to fairyland.

There is a considerable body of Celtic legend, too, which presents the fairies as dread creatures, soulless ones who sought power over men. Beautiful and terrible they are in such legends—"the slender women of the green kirtle and the yellow hair . . . the lordly ones of the hollow hills." And to fall into the power of such, was to be eternally trapped; divorced from the company of men, hidden from the sight of God.

Fairyland, in these aspects of folklore, was certainly neither a place reserved only for heroes and fair women, nor did the concept of being held there in thrall match that of willing entry into the joyousness of the legendary Otherworld. Yet still the time-scale of legend has to be remembered, for the belief preserved in both types of tale shows its later aspects. These were developing only very slowly over the long period it took for Christianity to gain final ascendancy over the former religions of Europe; and in this process, to absorb the motivating belief behind the Cult of the Dead into its own doctrine of the immortality of the soul. And so, even although folklore thus occasionally presents a confused picture of

this Otherworld, the different thought-strains caus-
ing the apparent confusion can still be traced.

In sum, then, the fairy, or Otherworld, is purely a
metaphysical concept, from which it would seem
logical to conclude that the fairies themselves are
only a product of the storyteller's imagination. Yet if
fairies are indeed no more than creatures of fantasy,
how may we account for *this* sort of tale—one which
comes from the Hebridean island of Pabbay, and is
only a single instance of many such stories?

There was a woman in Pabbay, it seems, and
she was the wife of the blacksmith there. She
had an iron pot, a good big one that was a real
treasure to her, and one day there comes to her
house a woman asking for a handful of meal and
a loan of this big iron pot. Herself could see that
this woman was one of the "daoine sidhe" [dun
shee], the People of Peace; and so she was not
willing to lend this treasure till she should find
what would come of the matter. She took the
meal, therefore, and she took the pot, and she
said to the Woman of Peace,

> *The smith is able to make;*
> *Cold iron hot with coal;*
> *The due of the pot is meat,*
> *And to bring it back again whole.*

The Woman of Peace was satisfied with this,
and the blacksmith's wife gave her the meal and
the pot. Off went the Woman of Peace, very

pleased, and when she brought the pot back again, it was full of meat. Herself was pleased then too, and the next time the Woman of Peace came asking for the meal and the pot, she gave them to her without any bother. But still she spoke her rhyme with the giving, and the Woman of Peace was satisfied with it; for still, when she brought the pot back again, it was full of meat. And so the two of them continued to oblige one another like this, until one day the blacksmith had a curiosity on him to find where his wife was getting the meat and who was this woman that was coming to his house.

Up on to the thatch he went the next time the Woman of Peace was coming to his house, and he peering down through the chimney hole to watch what was going on. In comes the Woman of Peace asking for the pot and the meal, and there was Herself handing them over and telling the rhyme about them. Right away then, the blacksmith knew it was a Woman of Peace had been borrowing the pot and bringing it back full of meat; and such a fright he got at this that he lost his grip on the thatch and fell down through the chimney hole into the fire. There was roaring and shouting from Himself then, and the Woman of Peace took great alarm at this. Off she ran, and she never came back again in life to borrow that pot.

This is a fairy story—although, on the surface, it is no more than an engaging little tale of two women reaching a comfortable domestic agreement, only to have it spoiled eventually by the clumsy curiosity of the husband of one of them. The clue to its real origin lies in the reference to the stranger woman as one of the "daoine sidhe," or People of Peace; the fairies having been thus named because it was the custom of Gaelic-speaking peoples to placate them with such flattering titles. And of course, the poor husband's clue to the woman's identity lay in the little scrap of homespun magic his wife used to protect the true ownership and to define the true value of the iron pot.

But note that the husband and the fairy woman were mutually afraid. And why, anyway, should a fairy want such mundane things as a handful of meal and an iron pot? Why was the pot such a precious article? And how was it that this fairy woman needed to borrow meal, yet could be so generous with meat? To answer such questions we must have a look at the anthropologists' theory on the origin of fairylore; and here again, we must relate verifiable fact to intelligent conjecture about Europe's remote past.

Fact lies in the gradual ascendancy of the new metal, iron, over the older alloy, bronze, for it was this which led to an eventual reshaping of prehistoric Europe's community patterns. Also, the most significant changes were those taking place in outlying areas of moor, bog, and forest where no cultivation had previously taken place, and where there could therefore be no growth of a settled population, with all the increasing sophistication of culture this implies.

Land-hungry tribes pushing west and north in successive waves over centuries of immigration had mastered the working of the new metal. Their agricultural habit, with its consequent variation of diet, had produced in them a taller, heavier breed than the pastoral tribes they began to displace. They had better weapons—an iron sword does not buckle under the force of a first blow, as bronze swords could, and did. But for all these superior physical attributes, they had one weakness. Because they were primitives, their belief in magic was as much a ruling force with them as it was with the small hunters and herdsmen they displaced; and in primitive societies, it is usual for the conqueror to regard the religion of the conquered as superior to his own in the arts of evil magic.

To relate fact to conjecture, therefore, we need only look at recurring elements in folklore to see strong supporting evidence of a gradual displacement of one people by another, with the smaller race eventually taking on the role of an unseen enemy operating a form of guerilla war on the fringes of the taller folks' settlements; yet still with both sides keeping up some degree of cautious communication with one another.

The smaller people, for instance, were of pastoral habit; and fairies always appear in story as having cattle, but no crops. Their homes are always said to be in "the middle earth," or in "the hollow hills"; and again, this is entirely consistent with the Bronze Age type of dwellings, which were beehive-shaped, sunk a few feet deep in the ground and roofed with turf; so that, when overgrown with long grass or heather, they had the appearance of hillocks. Their disposition was also very scattered, which indicates that each group of these dwellings would of necessity have its own ruler; and in terms of the social structure required to preserve the identity of very early nomadic tribes, this was likely to have been a "queen."

The small people of the middle earth, however, could not—originally, at least—have been markedly smaller than others. "He knew she was a woman of fairy," says one old story, "because of the colour of the gown she wore"; and folklore abounds in tales of such encounters, where fairies were only identified by some peculiarity of dress, or speech, or manner. Certainly the difference in height could not have been such as to rule out occasional intermarriage between the two peoples, as we can guess at from all the accounts of men winning fairy brides. The repeated motif of a mortal man marrying the fairy queen is a further indication of this, as well as something which lends colour to the guess at a matrilinear society in which the ruling female may wed as often and as variously as she chooses. But even more than that, it strikes the romantic note of love crossing all barriers, and it is on this note that we have not only some of the most beautiful of all fairy tales, but also the most revealing.

"True Thomas lay on Eildon bank," says the ballad form of one of these tales; "a ferlie spi'ed wi' his e'e."

89

A "ferlie," in the old Scots, is a wonder, or a marvel; and the marvel seen by True Thomas—the thirteenth-century Scottish poet, Thomas Learmonth of Ercildoune—was the Fairy Queen coming towards him along the bank of the Eildon River. With one kiss she woos him, wins him utterly, and for seven years he lives with her in Fairyland; but, at the end of that time, she tells him that this is when the fairies must "pay their teind tae hell." And this "teind," or rent, she fears, will be Thomas himself. Lovingly she sends him away, first laying the gift of truth on his tongue—much to his own dismay, as it happened; for, with truth always on his tongue, how will he ever be able to sell a horse or make love to a woman again?

Thus strangely, the man who had before been only Thomas the Rhymer became "True" Thomas—a poet who would thenceforth also be a prophet; and eventually there came a day when something even stranger happened to him. A white hart and a white hind were seen coming together out of the forest, and walking without fear towards his tower at Ercildoune. "It is a sign," said he, and rising from among his friends he went out to meet the beautiful, quiet creatures. They turned. All three walked back into the forest, and this "last outpassing through the fern curtain" was also the last glimpse of Thomas in this world.

How much is truth and how much is legend in this story? Ercildoune is the ancient version of the name Earlston, and the remains of the tower in which Thomas the Rhymer lived can still be seen near the modern town of that name. His poetry is still extant. Many of the prophecies that were said to have come from his gift of truth have been fulfilled; and even so late as the present century, one at least of them has come startlingly true. How much, then, was magical and how much was true about the fairies of folklore?

The stories one finds there do not credit them with being winged, as do modern tales. Even more romantically, they were reputed to be able to make themselves invisible and to ride on the wind; but against this one must set the prosaic facts that an exceptional fleetness of foot was essential to primitive hunters, and—as anyone who has tried to stalk a partridge along a winter furrow could tell—the art of camouflage can confer invisibility at will.

The characteristic weapon of the fairies was a flint arrowhead, thrown like a dart, or "spanged" between thumb and forefinger as a boy shoots a marble; and to be "elf-shot" in fairy tales was to be struck by one of these arrows. The result was paralysis, and always, eventually, death. Yet cattle which were elf-shot were only temporarily paralysed, and since these arrowheads were so small that they could cause only a minor wound, it is not unreasonable in the first place to suppose that the paralysis was caused by a poison of the curare type; and in the second place, that the recovery of the cattle was not simply due to their having a different-from-human metabolism, but also because they were not suggestible—as men were—to the idea of death.

Fairies, finally, were reputed to have a superstitious fear of iron, and to have no power against it. Iron was therefore *the* charm against them—remember Mr. Kirk's instruction that he could not escape the fairies' power unless a dirk, an iron knife, was thrown over his head. And here we come back full circle to the basis of the anthropologists' theory on the origins of fairylore, for the form of magic among primitives has always been the simple type known as sympathetic magic; the operative principle of which is that like must affect like. By definition, therefore, this theorises that an effect must resemble its cause; and so, the mere fact that the fairies were supposed to have no counter-charm to the power of iron argues that they possessed neither iron itself nor the means of working it.

By a curious quirk of circumstance too, it is the very persistence of belief in magic that has not only helped to keep alive the desire to believe in fairylore, but has also provided some of the most practical proof on the anthropologists' theory of its origins. Acceptance of the fairies as the superiors of mortals in the magic arts led to the argument that it would be only natural for witches to consult them in this practice; and the bones of such argument have been preserved in the records of numerous trials for witchcraft all over Europe, from early in the fifteenth to nearly the end of the seventeenth century. The most famous of these trials, of course, is that of Joan of Arc, in which much of the questioning which strove to show her a witch was directed to proving that she had trafficked in fairy magic or had been influenced by belief in fairies. The trial which provides most information on fairies as such, is that of Isobel Goudie of Auldearn, a village in the Scottish Highlands.

Isobel's trial took place in the year 1662, and the records show her as having made four separate and detailed statements to the court. She was not coerced into doing so, either by threats of any kind, or by physical torments. Indeed, she seems to have been one of those whose conscience weighed so heavy that she was eager to confess all her activities as a witch. Moreover, although the whole trial appears to the modern mind as a situation of complete fantasy, it is clear from these statements that she was a woman who persisted in describing something which has all the hallmarks of an actual experience. This, she claimed, took place both among and inside some mounds referred to as "the Downie Hills," which she said she had visited in company with other women from her village. This supposed witch coven was led by a man—conventionally always referred to in such cases as "the Devil"; and talking of what happened then, she says,

> I was in the Downie Hills, and got meat there from the Queen of Fairy, more than I could eat. The Queen of Fairy is brawly [beautifully] clothed in white linens and in brown and white clothes, and the King of Fairy is a braw man, well favoured and broad faced. There was elf bulls roaring and rioting up and down there, which frightened me. As for the elf arrowheads,

93

the Devil . . . delivers them to Elf boys who shape them with a sharp thing like a packing needle. The hill opened, and we came to a fair and large room in the day time. There are great bulls roaring about at the entry there, which frightened me.

This statement—which has necessarily been translated from the broad Scots dialect of the time—answers very clearly to the idea of fairies as they traditionally appear in folklore; mound-dwellers living some distance apart from the site of other settlement (from Auldearn, in this case) possessing cattle, having a "queen" as their ruling personage, and arrowheads as their weapons. Significantly also, although Isobel talks of the features, clothing, and activities of these mound-dwellers, she makes no mention of their physical size; and since her statement is otherwise so detailed, one could justifiably conclude that she found nothing about this worth noting.

The evidence of this and other trials, in effect, would seem to point to at least a vestigial and very scattered survival of the type of people who appear in folklore as "fairies." Yet still the anthropologists cannot have it all their own way, for although they can bring not only the woman of Pabbay to witness for them but also Isobel Goudie and her ilk, they still cannot have the white hart and the white hind which led True Thomas at his last outpassing through the fern curtain, the lordly ones of the hollow hills, and the ineffable beauty of the Land of Heart's Desire. There has to be an accommodation in this; for fairies, it would seem, are composite creatures, and belief in fairies is a composite matter. Some of its elements seem admittedly to have been born in fact. Some have sprung from high, poetic imagining; and it would be foolish to deny one at the expense of the other, for our culture is all the richer from the blend that has resulted.

There is a most exquisite example of this, indeed, which—like the fetch of Mr. Kirk—can be "visibly seen" in Dunvegan Castle, the home of the Chief of Clan McLeod, on the Hebridean island of Skye. There is much fairylore in these islands, and some of this concerns the ability of fairy women—again to quote from the story of Mr. Kirk, but this time in the very words of his *Secret Commonwealth*—"to spin very fine, to dye, to tissue, and embroider." The music of the fairies is also said to be of a strange and exceptional sweetness—indeed, some of the songs of the Hebrides are said to have been taught to a mortal girl by her fairy lover—and these two talents of fairy come together in the story of a certain Lady wife of a Chief of McLeod.

This Lady of McLeod, the story goes, was startled to hear one day a sweet, strange singing from the room where her infant son lay asleep in his cradle. She hurried towards the sound, and was even more startled to see a small woman in a green kirtle, singing as she rocked the cradle and smoothed a silken banner over the infant it held.

"God sain us!" cried the Lady in alarm, and immediately on these words of Christian blessing, the small woman vanished. But she left the memory of her song behind her, and she also left the silken banner, which hangs to this day on a wall of Dunvegan Castle. The colour of it (as I remember from my last sight of it) is the palest gold. The texture is almost incredibly fine, and it glistens as it hangs there, like a great, gold, glowing cobweb. To look at it is to wonder, and to *want* to believe in everything that reason says cannot be so; and paradoxically, this is the ultimate in reason, for it would be either a very stupid, or overbold, or inconceivably clever person who could accept or assert that the world consists only of what we can appreciate with our five senses.

A minority of people might be thus dogmatic, but even the scientist of modern times is gradually being forced into the position where he must admit the existence of phenomena which are not subject to known laws. The title of precognitive telepathy, for instance, has been given to the Scottish Highlander's anciently-known second sight. Experiments are carried out to test its incidence in representative samples of a population; but, as Mr. Robert Kirk could have told the experimenters, the door of the Otherworld cannot be thus crudely breached. Himself a man with much experience of the workings of that phenomenon, he writes gravely in his *Secret Commonwealth,*

"The men of that Second Sight do not discover strange Things when asked, but at Fits and Raptures, as if inspired by some Genius at that Instant, which did before lurk in or about them."

Even for the person not so gifted, however, there can be an indication of such "Fits and Raptures"; for most of us at some time or another have had a feeling of *something* we cannot name—a fleeting sense of anticipation, perhaps, that has no apparent relation to events, a glimpse of something that could not possibly exist, the sense of a sound beyond hearing—and for the moment that this lasts, it seems, we are trembling on the brink of discovery. This could be mere atavism, a brief reversion to the type of primitive creature we once were, but that still does not negate the feelings themselves or prove they did not have a cause. For all we can argue to the contrary, the vision beyond sight may still be there, the sound beyond hearing may still exist. The men who conceived of an Otherworld interpenetrating with the world of our five senses may have been right after all; and the irony of modern and so-called rational attempts to refute their concept shows in the vague aftermath of disappointment when we realise we have, in fact, heard nothing, seen nothing. Everything is as it was before; definable, explicable, quantifiable. And the magic, which for that fleeting moment seemed imminent, has not happened after all.

The fascination that fairy stories hold for children is rooted in this same feeling; for childhood is the time when the capacity to think that the supernatural may exist touches the point of believing, or actively wishing to believe that it does so. Childhood is the time when we are more sensitive to atmosphere than at any other period in our lives, when our senses are undimmed, when we respond primarily to emotion rather than to thought. It is the time when we rely on ritual, pattern, and order; for a child's world has small bounds, and to feel secure, he must know what these bounds are. To be master in his world he must have a formula which controls all that operates within it.

Thus childhood is also quite literally the time of magic, for all magic is based on a recognition of pattern and order in the universe. And since its purpose is to bring about some marvellous result by reshaping part of that order, there must similarly be pattern and order in its methods. A formula for this must be created; a ritual invented for dispensing the formula. From the form and rhythm thus achieved will spring the new, marvellous order—the magic; and it is because of their own need for pattern, order, and ritual that children are instinctively aware of this.

The rhymes, the games, the obsessions of childhood all show this awareness. A child walking alongside a fenced garden will religiously touch every seventh railing as he passes. A small girl bouncing a ball chants a rhyme like an invocation to keep it balanced in mid-air. A group of children playing will pattern their game on an ordered sequence, invoke numbers, chant incantatory phrases—all with the sense that these are the key to everything happening as they *want* it to happen. And when it comes to magic in a story, they have no difficulty in accepting either the magic itself or the conditions attaching to its effect. Indeed, so accustomed are children to the instinctively assumed effect of their own uses of ritual and formula, that it would come as more of a surprise to them if there was no magical solution to a difficult story situation.

Children are in sympathy with magic, in effect, in much the same way as magic itself was supposed to spring from a sympathetic interaction of force on force, or object on object; and so, for this period of life, at least, it could be said that fairy stories are a necessary satisfaction. But not fairy stories in the debased form which threatens to trivialise them out of existence altogether. To present children with this poor, thin food for their imaginations is to starve them both of the strong, homely fare provided in the folklore of small domestic transactions between "fairies" and humans, and also of the rich romanticism of ancient legend. There are implications beyond this also, for the trivial presentation of fairy stories is far from the comparatively harmless matter it might seem to be.

It owes nothing to the grass roots of superstition, and so it cannot touch the powerful springs of emotion in a child's mind. It glosses over the sharp terrors of the truly unknown—which is the unknowable— and so it does nothing to counterbalance the child's equally sharp apprehension of these terrors. It is ignorant of the timeless yearning of humans to identify with their sense of an eternal oneness in the universe —the sense which tells man he has a soul; and so it can convey nothing of the comparable timelessness of the struggle between this sense and the temptation to enter the charmed world of fairyland where that soul will be eternally lost. It is just as ignorant of the opposite form of belief which presents the fairy world as man's picture of the vanished golden age of his own world, and so it offers nothing to the opposite yearning which has created this picture.

It makes no use of laughter, and thus displays its final poverty; for although the human capacity to react in laughter has achieved the appearance of spontaneity, it is still a form of self-mockery rooted in fear. And in the running conflict where laughter springs from the battle between man's wit and fairy magic, the fairy stories of folklore recognise both the roots and the development of this reaction.

These are all serious deprivations in the reading of young children, for the things they represent are constants in human nature and are just as much a part of the child's makeup—in some respects more so —as that of the adult. The fact that children are unable to define them is not relevant to the present argument, for that is the task of the writer, who must be capable of working at two levels—that of a simple story which can immediately be grasped by a young reader, and a deeper level which makes use of symbolism to convey the deeper implications of the story. Achievement of these two levels, moreover, depends almost as much as poetry does on a choice of words which will be precise in meaning yet subtle in effect, and on the rhythmic and cadenced use of these words. The writer who cannot deploy his medium in this way has therefore no business to be writing fairy stories at all; for, by doing so, he is inflicting on his young readers a last, serious deprivation—the loss of a rich experience in language.

All my working life as a children's writer I have battled against such a situation, and this is not simply because of a scholarly interest in the origins of fairylore. It is also because I am deeply aware of that something in all of us which creates the need for fairy stories in childhood—a feeling so strong that it lingers into our adult life and stays there in some form or another to the end of our days. The thread of it runs through all our literature in the form of longing for mankind's mythical "golden age":

> *When all the world was young, lad,*
> *And all the grass was green,*
> *And every goose a swan, lad,*
> *And every lass a queen . . .*

Thus Charles Kingsley singing of youth's vanished years, and equating them with that golden time.

> *And still it half calls up the realm of fairy,*
> *Where I beheld what never was to be . . .*

Thus Byron, in lines that give voice to the haunting ache of this something in us all; the feeling that some time some where was a perfect world that held no pain, no anger, no cruelty, where death itself had been conquered: that we knew this world, and have somehow mysteriously forgotten how to reach it again.

The pure charm of everything summed up in the word "magic" is a reflection of this feeling. That I know, in the same way as I know when a note is struck in tune. And one thing more I know, I can only describe by telling of a certain effect one may see on summer evenings in the Highlands of Scotland when the sun has gone down behind the mountains, but is still striking shafts of light up into the small clouds floating above their crests.

These clouds look like golden islands then, floating just beyond the misty blue-green horizon made by the tops of the high bens; and maybe this is why legend has it that Tir nan Og, the Land of Heart's Desire, lies in the west and can only be glimpsed by living sight for a few moments at sunset. Maybe it is the reason, I say, for although one can guess at such a thing, one can never truly know it.

But what I do know is that to look at this sight is to feel a catch at the heart and a great longing for something you cannot name—something irremediably lost, but so beautiful you would give your soul to discover it again. And beyond a doubt, I know then also that although this feeling is many centuries old it has as many centuries still to run, and that fairy stories will last so long as men live. For it is just so long as this also that some of them at least will continue to look longingly into the west for their own brief glimpse of Tir nan Og.

The Limits
of Language

I have a brother who enjoys illustrating a point with gems of so-called Irish philosophy, and a recent one in this vein runs,

"Sure, when one door shuts, another one closes."

The meaning comes over, despite the confusion in semantics. If one thing doesn't work for you, there's always an alternative; and in considering the limits of language, this is particularly true of writing for children. The mere inexperience of one's readers may sometimes rule out the more sophisticated forms of expression, but a simpler choice is always available. Added to which, this alternative may even better serve the purpose of language by being still more powerful or more pointed in its reference.

"I'm famished," for example, might well be beyond a very young reader's vocabulary. "I'm so hungry I could eat a horse" would be a simple alternative which gives the same degree of exaggeration, and—depending on context—could add either drama or humour to the situation.

In terms of creative writing, indeed, the scope of language is infinitely variable, its possibilities equally so. Only its limits are arguable—and once again, never more so than in writing for children. Profanity, for instance—what about that? Well, *what* about it? When I was small, my Presbyterian grannie had ideas on the subject! If I said, "Good gracious!" she pounced immediately with the question, "Who is Gracious, and who is Good?" And for that particular piece of profanity, my punishment was to repeat aloud the Third Commandment—"Thou shalt not take the name of the Lord thy God in vain. . . ."

Reading the novels of Alexandre Dumas a few years later, I found it odd—and still do—that "*Mon Dieu!*" was permissible in reading, and "My God!" still punishable in speech. (Incidentally, also, this was my first muted contact with what I was later to recognise as the double standard that induces publishers to burst out into a foreign tongue in passages where the law of their own country might catch up with them.)

It might not be unfair also to point out that the child who innocently—and quite acceptably—exclaims "jeez!" is very probably using a corrupted form of "Jesus," in the same way as "bloody" is a corruption of "By Our Lady." The varying degrees of profanity, indeed, are so much a part of accepted speech that the writer's entitlement is to express them in any way he thinks consistent with that of the character involved—which means there is no reason whatsoever why "Goddamit" should not have equal rights with D'Artagnan's *"Mon Dieu!"* or *"sacre coeur!"*

Obscenity . . . ? It would be going too far, surely, to permit that—except that this is not the point on which the argument turns. Profanity is an offence against an abstract concept, held dear by some, and by others considered invalid. Its significance is therefore much open to doubt; but the very pointed significance of obscenity lies in its being an offence against the personality of both speaker and hearer. In literary context, also, it is too restricted in expression to be anything but boring, and there are much more effective ways of indicating it than merely recording its content. Both objections, in any case, imply the imposition of moral as opposed to linguistic limits; and to advance the proper exploration of these latter, one might look next at the rhythmic possibilities of language.

Here again there is advantage for the simpler form of words, the sophisticated forms tending to have the complex structure which may well be rhythmically awkward. Simple words, on the other hand, can be built smoothly and musically into the rhythmic sequence which is a natural setting for some bright, flashing fragment of poetry. This was the art of words as practised by the tellers of folktales; and although folktales were not composed for an audience of children, it is their lasting delight for the young reader that has enabled the secret of this art to be transmitted.

Then he went in at the door of that house, the tall and dark door that was guarded by a great, black dog with eyes burning red as hot coals, and teeth like white, sharp knives. He was tall, yet still not tall against the high darkness of that door. The dog looked at him as he passed. He looked at the dog, and knew the white, sharp knives of its teeth could draw blood from him as richly red as its burning eyes. But a spell was on the creature, and the spell would not let it move. And so he came safely, at last, into that house.

This is not an extract from any folktale. It is simply an exercise in the style of the folktale that takes simple, vivid words and builds them in repeated and contrasted sequence to achieve an inevitable rhythmic pattern. Most of these words have only one syllable, but every syllable has been placed to reflect with maximum impact off another. The ordering of the phrases has been carefully achieved—"white, sharp knives," for instance, being preferable on several counts to "sharp, white knives."

The latter use is commonplace, almost a cliché. Also, "sharp, white knives" requires the whole phrase to be read before the idea of teeth as knives can be taken in; and there is a further loss of effect in the interposing of "white" between "sharp" and "knives."

In "white, sharp knives," on the other hand, the sequence of description allows for perfect coordination of eye and brain, and therefore achieves the maximum impact from the same idea. The use of "white" initially also relates immediately by contrast to "black" in the description of the dog, and thus there is instant pointing of the rhythmic balance in "great, black dog" and "white, sharp knives."

The whole passage could be analysed in the same way to prove my point about the rhythmic power of simple language. Yet none of this would touch the springs of composition, any more than one could hope to paint the effect of sunshine on a tree by making a quantitative calculation of light. There is an X factor in this—the creative element which derives from the writer's sense of the magic in words. Nor is there anything rhetorical in the use of that phrase "the magic of words."

Once upon a time everybody believed in magic— and that phrase is not the gambit of a children's writer attempting to stretch analogy by means of a technique of her own craft. No-one has yet devised a phrase more evocative than *Once upon a time . . . ,* and the belief underlying the practice of magic has a direct bearing on the whole concept of language.

To proceed in sober truth, then, with this once upon a time— In every act of magic there are two elements. These are the Rite, which is a set of actions performed according to a specific ritual; and the Spell, consisting of words uttered according to a formula. The actions of the Rite are designed to convey the magic, and so to cast its power on the person or object to be affected by it; but the magic itself—and with good reason—is contained in the Spell.

The meaning of every word, it is argued, is innate to its sound and structure. Thus the word itself is the essence of what it names; and to capture that essence in speech is to be able to direct its power to a desired end.

The word "leaf," for instance—to give the most random illustration of this theory—is more than a label for some fragment of vegetable matter. Beyond this it holds everything essentially understood by the "leafness" of leaf—colour, shape, texture, positioning in relation to stem, twig, branch, root, the idea of burgeoning, growth, decay, eventual resumption into its organic source; and thus, finally, the innate meaning of its sound relates directly to the hidden life-force which has generated both the idea of leaf and the word which expresses it.

Thus also, there is apparently mystical significance in words which makes them, themselves, inherently magical. Nor need the power of one word ever stand alone. To build "leaf" into "rustle of leaf" projects connotations of meaning that range from the minute whispering of one tiny leaf against another, to all the sound and movement of some great Aeolian harp of leaves. And so the magician may join word with word in endless permutations of power, with the strength of the resulting Spell depending solely on his own skill in devising the formula that will express the accumulated power of their inherent magic.

There is a terrible, yet somehow thrilling arrogance to all this, for the mere existence of magic recognises an established pattern of order in the universe—the aim of even the smallest act of magic being marvellously to alter some aspect of that pattern. The power the magician seeks is therefore limitless; and if words are to be the tool he uses both to achieve and exercise that power, it argues as a central principle that there can be no limit either to their power. Yet words are a product of the human mind which is itself limited in capacity; and herein rests the problem which is as much the burden of the creative writer as it is that of the magician.

The aim the writer sets himself is the same as that of the magician—to penetrate to the secret, beating heart of life; and by touching it, marvellously to transmute one set of circumstances to another. His method is the same. Instinctually he senses that words are inherently magical, and that by setting one with another he may formulate the language which is his spell. Yet intellectually he is aware that words may be defined only to the extent of ensuring their correct use in context, and all creative writing is an attempt to solve the contradiction this imposes.

In the work of the children's writer, also, there must always be a delicate balance held between the intellectual and the instinctual approach to words— childhood itself being that highly-specialised time when language has as much novelty to emotional and physical experience as to the intellectual. The small child, particularly, relates novel perception so closely to the concept of language that his grasp on the inherent magic of words could also be argued as instinctual.

"Up!" cries the genial adult, swinging a small child

into the air; and laughing, the child registers the sound of the word in terms of everything intrinsic to this new dimension of "up." The small child sees something that delights his eye. He smiles, stretching a hand towards this visual pleasure. "Pretty," agrees the genial adult, and so supplies a sound which, to that child's ear, is inherent with all those agreeable qualities stimulating his visual sense.

Further to this, also, those earliest perceptions of word-magic are reinforced by adult enjoyment of a child's pleased reaction to everything that seems to be magical. Even a game of peekaboo with a baby falls into this category, the baby shrieking with laughter at the adult face popping into view and then magically disappearing to pop up again in another place, the adult delighted with the effect of this simple trick. The child so conditioned may later watch a conjurer performing his tricks. He hears *Hey Presto* as the rabbit is drawn out of the hat, and all previous experience induces him to associate the words with their seemingly magical result.

The Rite and the Spell have a long lineage—which gives them a stronger grip on our mental processes than we may have believed possible. Indeed, the strength is such that even the rational adult may revert at times to the child's instinctive process of association, and I well recall an experience which caused me this momentary reversion.

It was April, and a day of swift, sudden showers, with moments of calm sunshine between. Walking with my then four-year-old son, I thought to amuse him by claiming I could make it rain. I watched the misty movement of the rain-curtain on the hills, timed the arrival of the next shower, and shouted,

"*Abracadabra!*"

Instantly there was rain, and astonished laughter from the child.

"Turn it off too," he commanded, testing me.

I managed to time the word appropriately again; and so, magically making it rain and turning off the rain again, I beguiled the road home.

We reached the house seconds ahead of a shower of hail that came utterly unheralded by any warning sign, and at the same time the child decided to make his own attempt at magic. Turning at the door he looked up into the sky's blue and empty nothingness.

"*Abracadabra!*" Gaily he shouted the word, and with almost incredible violence, the hail erupted.

The child wailed his terror at this. The magic had gone wrong, and *he* had made it go wrong. This was angry magic, angry with him, and I was the only one who could stop it. I closed doors and windows against the hail, drew the curtains, putting the closed comfort of the house around him, but all to no purpose. In terror still he begged me to say the magic word again. *He* was afraid to try, in case something even worse happened. But I could do it—I *must* do it, or the hail would never go away.

There was nothing else for it but to say the word until my voice gave out or until the hail stopped, leaving fortune to dictate which would be the sooner. I went to the door, he clinging fearfully to my skirt. I shouted *"abracadabra!"* into the very face of the storm, and the hail stopped as abruptly as if it had been flicked off by a switch.

I looked down at the child. Huge, dark eyes, solemn with wonder, met my gaze; but they could be no more solemn than my own, I thought; for even although my reason informed me that the moment of switch-off had been a one-in-a-million coincidence, that moment had still touched me with a thrill that was wholly atavistic. And all through uttering a word. ... Yet still, I argued, this had been no ordinary word, for of all those I could have chosen, this was the very one anciently invented to give limitless power through limitless permutation of its letters.

So, on a personal level, I was affected by this experience; but there was a further dimension to it—a professional one, for the word involved was also one of those that mark the point where magician and writer part company in their attempts to solve the contradiction imposed by the limits of language.

Each deploys a finite method to an infinite aim, but the magician is an esoteric figure—part priest, part philosopher, part artist. It is not required of him to explain the deep meaning behind the apparent nonsense of words like "abracadabra," and thus his method may include aspects of language outside the comprehension of the common herd.

The function of the writer is not thus divided. He has a single-minded desire—to communicate; and to fulfil this desire, his use of language must answer to the degree of comprehension reasonably supposed for his readers. Not that this rules out inventiveness; nor, of course, does it dismiss nonsense *per se.* Context is the safety net here—as, for instance—when Lewis Carroll wrote:

> *'Twas brillig, and the slithy toves*
> *Did gyre and gimble in the wabe. . . .*

Six out of these thirteen words are utter nonsense, but the context clearly shows the time concerned—"brillig," the characters involved—"slithy toves," the actions of these characters—"gyre and gimble," and the place where all this happened—"the wabe." Thus, by one brilliant stroke of inventiveness, the writer has used word-nonsense to create a factual, and therefore understandable, situation.

So, in this respect, the writer may turn apparent disadvantage to positive asset in pursuing his own resolution to the contradiction between aim and method; with only the kind of writing on which he is engaged conditioning any expression of his feeling for the inherent magic of words. So, with the technique of his art, he may create the path that enables others to follow in his exploration to the limits of language.

Rhythm, simplicity, the word exactly right in context—these are the guidelines the children's writer must set on this path. But with all these, it has to be admitted, poetry has the advantage over prose; and calling on personal experience again to demonstrate this, I well remember how my infant heart wept over

Ralph Hodgson's poem "The Bells of Heaven," with its pitiful pictures of

> . . . *tamed and shabby tigers,*
> *And dogs and dancing bears,*
> *And wretched blind pit ponies,*
> *And little hunted hares.*

A few years later the poetry of G.K. Chesterton swept like some exuberant comet across my mind; and I was there with him at Lepanto, in the poem that describes the great sea-battle of that name. I was stumbling across the bloody deck of a galley, axe in hand, a terrible pity in my heart for the slaves trapped below that deck. And I swung that axe, crashing it down in the first blow for their freedom with a force of words, words, words. . . .

Scarlet running over on the silvers and the golds,
Breaking of the hatches up and bursting of the
> *holds,*
Thronging of the thousands up that labour under
> *sea,*
White for bliss and blind for sun and stunned for
> *liberty.*

What vitality! What rhythmic power! What utter rightness of simple words—those slaves held in darkness, suddenly freed into fierce sunlight—"*white . . . blind . . . stunned . . .*"

Never tell me there is a child anywhere who would

not respond to the bright blaze of this verse! From the inherent force of every significant word to the reflecting power of one word on another, it holds the true, the limitless capacity of magic to evolve marvellously its own unique pattern. But every coin has two sides, of course, and the other side of this coin is that magic is not confined to simple words.

There may be a thousand of these which can easily convey a meaning to a young reader, but only one other which is beautifully, brilliantly right in that particular context; and that other may well have subtleties beyond the reader's intellectual experience. This is where the children's writer has to continue with trusting his own feeling for words, and has also to start trusting his readers. If there are some of these who do not grasp the meaning from its context, there will also be some who have recourse to a dictionary, and some—the ones most like himself—who will take in the sense of the word almost by a process of osmosis. The important thing to be realised by adults outwith this experience is that the creative writer is not a sociologist, or an educator, nor yet anyone's hired hack; and if he has the ability to pierce further yet towards that true force of magic, he must not be expected to make do with a mere conjuring trick.

There is a question of insight involved here, and only the writer can tell why that one word is the only one for that particular context. He could hear it as striking a note of music peculiar to itself, yet utterly in tune with the whole music in his words. By contrast with an unremarkable setting, he could see it sparkle with all the brilliance of a suddenly-discovered jewel. It could be part of a pattern of sound and structure which nothing else could so well complete. It could be a word of ethnic significance, enriching dialogue or narrative drawn from the writer's native culture.

Insofar as creative writing can be analysed, all these are constituent factors of a prime importance, and all writers could throw light on them. All children's writers could speak to their additional importance in the reading experience of young people; but so far as the last-mentioned one is concerned—the enriching effect of words with ethnic significance—it may be that no-one is better placed to discuss this than the native-born Scottish writer.

This is no more than a matter of historical circumstance, of course, and certainly nothing which should make a Scot like myself "craw sae croose." This latter phrase is the equivalent of the English "to boast," and is drawn from the Doric—the dialect tongue of the Scottish Lowlands. Together with the standard English, which is the speech common to the whole of Scotland, and the Gaelic spoken in the Highlands, this gives the Scottish writer the possibly unique privilege of three languages on which to draw. And even although most Scots are fluent only in either Doric or Gaelic in addition to their standard English, the popular use of this latter still draws generously on both the older tongues. Where Doric is concerned, also, the cultural value becomes self-evident when it is realised that thousands of words from this dialect have very much wider connotations than their nearest English equivalent, and even a laboured explanation of these may be only approximate to their full meaning.

"Dreich" for example, describes a day which is grey, drizzly, overcast; but to say to one's neighbour, "Och, it's a dreich day," may be more than a comment on the weather. A dreich day may also be one which holds something sorrowful, an implication of something to damp the spirit. The implication is stated explicitly when one describes a person of melancholy temperament as "a dreich sort of body," or if one is told that the sermon the minister preached was "gey dreich."

"Fushionless" is another of those words of diverse meaning. It can be used of someone who does things in an uncoordinated way, or a handless sort of creature, or one who has very little sense of purpose in life. In its broadest sense, it can also be applied to someone whom life itself has defeated, who simply lacks any natural ability to cope with normal circumstances.

"Ach, Sheriff, he's juist a puir fushionless body."

This was the defence plea made recently in a Scottish court by counsel deserting his standard English in favour of the more descriptive Doric. "Remanded for background report," returned the Sheriff, recognising instantly from this that counsel's client was just another of those pieces of human flotsam—an exchange of verdict which saved both counsel and sheriff all the usual legal verbiage.

117

There is a humour and strength in Doric also, which is lacking in standard English. Who, for instance, would not prefer the comical sound of "tapselteerie" to the dull utility of "turned upside down"? How weak is the phrase "it makes you shiver," placed alongside the dark strength of "it gars ye grue"! And where standard English may state coldly of a youngster's tears, "I was sorry for the child," the Doric creates tender warmth from "My hert was sair for the bairn." (My heart was sore for the child.)

Where Doric may be flexible, robust, humorous, or warm in sentiment as compared to English, the outstanding quality of Gaelic is the music it conveys. The native Gaelic speaker, moreover, always tends to speak English in literal translation from the very different syntax of his own language, so that all the cadences of that tongue are retained in his English speech. Even in such commonplace matters as a comment on the weather, for instance, a Gaelic speaker would never say,

"It's a lovely day."

"It's beautiful weather that's in it." This would be his phrasing; and of course he would render the words in the softly-slurred consonants and liquid vowel sounds which are also part of the music of Gaelic speech.

This music on the tongue of the Gaelic speaker is matched by an inherent feeling for poetry, so that instinctively he projects this also into his uses of English. "But still the blood is strong, the heart is Highland," says the exile's poem, "And we in dreams behold the Hebrides." A Gaelic speaker would not say he was intensely moved by the sad beauty of these lines. He would say,

"The heart in me is breaking for them."

An additional feature of Gaelic lies in the fact of its being an ancient language relating to a way of life now almost vanished; with the result that it contains no synonyms for modern artefacts or usages. The Highlander, however, has a vein of sly humour in his nature, so that his invention of equivalent terms holds many a quiet joke at the expense of modern times—the best of all these, to my mind, being his phrase for the system of credit purchase. This, in the Gaelic, exposes the whole farce of modern economics to a peculiarly pointed ridicule, for in this language it is known simply as "empty-handed money."

There is a tremendous heritage implied in all this, and no-one worthy the name of writer could fail in wanting to draw on its riches. Yet merely to pepper a text with words in a language unknown to the reader is a form of snobbery from any writer; and the effect can range from amused recognition of this *as* snobbery to frustration at having some part of a vital meaning obscured. The young reader accustomed only to an English or American vocabulary is left with the feeling of bafflement which in children is the first step to boredom; and so, inevitably, the writer has to find a way of explaining the unfamiliar words.

The technicalities of this are simple, and rest

mainly on the use of reflected meaning, either in the dialogue or in the enveloping narrative. . . .

The children by this time were all shivering with cold. The woman of the house built the fire to a good, roaring blaze, and they crouched down close to the flames, each one huddling into himself and into the group. The woman smiled to see this.

"That's the way," she said kindly. "Coorie doon thegither, beside the warm."

Coorie doon . . . Any other words are harsh beside these gentle, homely sounds! No wonder that one of the oldest and sweetest of Scots lullabies is made from just these two words, repeated over and over. The inherent magic of words becomes apparent, also, in the way that "coorie" captures the idea of curling small into oneself; and to call a fire "the warm" is coming very close to making an act of magic, for this word names the one quality that captures the essential "fireness" of fire.

The technical simplicity of this, however, masks the real problem the writer faces in making the widest possible use of words. The original intention must be kept firmly in mind, for one is not—or should not be—writing to demonstrate a mastery of these. Yet a passion for words may easily bewitch the writer into this trap, and once it springs on him—there is the end to all pushing forward in exploring the limits of language! No frontiers can be descried from within

120

a trap—least of all that one which must be crossed before the contradiction in all creative writing can be solved.

What happens when this frontier *is* crossed has no real name, although some of us call it inspiration and seek it wildly under that name. It involves a shift in focus on the whole idea of language—a sudden shift, and only a slight one, but suddenly also then, the writer has the final spell that touches the secret life-force unifying the temporal with the eternal; for when the shift happens is when language becomes a concept which is somehow greater than itself.

It happened with Shelley when he pierced far enough beyond the frontier to write, "Life, like a dome of many-coloured glass, stains the white radiance of Eternity." John Donne crossed the frontier with the statement, "I am involved in mankind." William Dunbar ventured across it with "Lament for the Makaris," the poem that set his own tremendous fear of death against an even more tremendous roll-call of all the dead who had once been the lovely poets of life.

Each of these writers, named at random here, realised in language that concept which is greater than itself. Behind them stand the countless others who, in some form of words or another, have reached that same far frontier of realisation. Yet much agony of spirit has attended all the journeying there, and sometimes it can happen that the child's way towards it is an easier one.

"He went back through the Wet Wild Woods, waving his wild tail, and walking by his wild lone. But he never told anybody."

The child who reads these lines by Rudyard Kipling will recognise instantly the magic of all creatures living free in secret places. Instantly also, then, he will have the spell that binds his human to their creature essence, and this will take him more than halfway to the deepest secret of that final spell. But whether or not he ever realises this in childhood, the direction to it will have been set by his early, near-instinctual grasp on the magic of words. The way will be further opened up by his automatic association of the Rite with the Spell, and all his reading will lead him on—either to a small or large extent—in what will eventually be his own, conscious exploration to the limits of language.

Fortunate the child encouraged in this—and I may speak with feeling here, not only as a children's writer, but as one who was so encouraged.

Long ago I had for schoolmaster a person who was a fine scholar, a great teacher, and a man of warm humanity. He loved words—even a child younger than I was then could have seen that. But the really wonderful thing about this teacher was his enormous *respect* for language. This was what I sensed in him as a child; and what finally became the sum of all I learned from him was to have that same respect. This also is what lies behind the solution to that contradiction which equally faces the magician and the creative writer; and thus it explains why the magician fails to find that solution where the writer may succeed in doing so.

Words are the magician's slaves, to be coerced, commanded to the inglorious end of bringing power or satisfying curiosity. But glory cannot be impelled from inglory, and so no-one can force words to yield their ultimate magic. The writer who loves and respects language understands this. Words are not slaves to him, but dear companions, and what he learns from them at last is that the frontier he tries so hard to reach lies within himself. The answer to the contradiction posed by the limits of language is in his own soul.

This is glory, freely descending; the unnameable thing that happens, finding its own name. And this *is* that ultimate magic.

Selected
Bibliography

Bailey, Patrick. *Orkney.* Newton Abbot, England: David & Charles, 1971; *also* North Pomfret, Vermont: David & Charles, 1974.

Burt. *Letters from a Gentleman.* Edinburgh: Oliver & Boyd, 1822, from Burt, *Letters,* 1726.

Campbell, J.F. *Popular Tales of the West Highlands.* 4 vols. Paisley, Scotland, and London: Gardner, 1890.

Cruden, Stewart. *The Scottish Castle.* London: Thomas Nelson & Sons, 1963.

de Johnstone, Chevalier. *A Memoir of the 'Forty-Five.* London: Folio Society, 1940 and 1958, from publication of 1820, from manuscript in museum of Clan MacPherson Society, Newtonmore.

Forbes, Bishop. *The Lyon in Mourning.* 4 vols. Papers relative to the affairs of Prince Charles Edward Stuart. Edinburgh: Scottish History Society, 1895.

Kirk, Robert. *The Secret Commonwealth of Elves, Fauns, and Fairies.* Stirling, Scotland: Eneas Mackay, 1933, from manuscript of 1691.

Linklater, Eric, *Orkney and Shetland.* 2nd ed. London: Robert Hale, 1971; *also* New York: International Publications Service, 1971.

MacKenzie, Agnes Mure. *Scottish Pageant.* 4 vols. Edinburgh: Oliver & Boyd, 1946–50.

McNeill, F. Marian. *The Silver Bough.* 4 vols. Glasgow: William MacLellan, 1957–68.

Malleus Maleficarum. 1486. Reprint. London: Folio Society, 1968.

Murray, Margaret. *The Witch Cult in Western Europe.* Oxford, England: Clarendon Press, 1962; *also* New York: Oxford University Press, 1962.

Nicholson, James R. *Shetland.* Newton Abbot, England: David & Charles, 1972; *also* North Pomfret, Vermont: David & Charles, 1972.

Piggott, Stuart. *The Druids.* London: Thames & Hudson, 1968; *also* New York: Praeger, 1968.

Pitcairn, Robert. *Ancient Criminal Trials.* 4 vols. Edinburgh, 1833; *also* reprinted as *Ancient Criminal Trials in Scotland.* 4 vols. New York: AMS Press.

Ross, Anne. *Everyday Life of the Pagan Celts.* New York: G.P. Putnam's Sons, 1970; Carousel ed., 1972.

Scot, Reginald. *The Discoverie of Witchcraft.* 1584. Reprint. Carbondale, Illinois: Southern Illinois University Press, Centaur Classics, 1964; *also* reprint. New York: Da Capo Press.

Scott, Sir Walter. *Letters on Demonology and Witch-

craft. London: John Murray, 1830; *also* reprint of 1887 ed. R. West.

Sharpe, Charles Kirkpatrick. *Historical Account of the Belief in Witchcraft in Scotland.* London and Glasgow, 1884; *also* reprint. Singing Tree, 1974.

Simpson, W. Douglas. *The Ancient Stones of Scotland.* London: Robert Hale, 1969.

About the Author

MOLLIE HUNTER is the author of many popular and acclaimed books for young people. She loves to write about the people of her native Scotland—from the distant history of THE STRONGHOLD, which won the 1974 Carnegie Medal (the British equivalent of the Newbery Medal), to recollections of her own young adult years, reflected in A SOUND OF CHARIOTS and its sequel, HOLD ON TO LOVE. Her most recent book, THE MERMAID SUMMER, makes no mention of time or place, but is steeped in the magic of the Scottish folklore tradition that Hunter knows so well.

Born in East Lothian of a Scots mother and an Irish father, Mollie Hunter has said she never wanted to be anything but a writer. Her wish came true; as one distinguished American critic proclaimed, she is "Scotland's most gifted storyteller." In addition to her books for children, she has written several one-act plays, published in Great Britain, and articles on Scots history which have appeared in *The Glasgow Herald* and *The Scotsman*. In 1975 she was chosen to deliver the sixth annual May Hill Arbuthnot Honor Lecture at the University of Pennsylvania; it was this lecture that both inspired and formed the basis for TALENT IS NOT ENOUGH.

Mollie Hunter now lives in a Highland glen near Inverness with her husband, Michael. There she writes, gardens, and tells marvelous stories to her grandchildren.